MoneySmart™

Personal Finance Workbook

Do Something Smart
With Your Money™

David A. Pandone

This work was printed and distributed by:

CreateSpace

a DBA of On-Demand Publishing LLC

part of the Amazon group of companies.

Do Something Smart With Your Money Publications

A division of SunCountry Property, Phoenix, Arizona

ISBN: 0615585086

ISBN-13: 978-0615585086

DEDICATION

For my father, Don Pandone; a man loved by many for his warmth and wisdom;
You are missed by all who knew you, especially your son.

CONTENTS

ACKNOWLEDGMENTS

I'd like to thank my Heavenly Father for the strength and determination to complete this work. "May it be a blessing to your many faithful children who are today in bondage; held by unseen chains. Bless and protect it from those who would seek to keep them bound." I'm also grateful for the small slices of wisdom with which he's seen fit to bless me from time to time. It is a gift I prayed for long ago, when I was very young.

I'd like to thank Chris Chandler, my first mentor in this arena, for going above and beyond our business relationship to help get me started on budgeting my personal finances so many years ago. I learned much that I still use while sitting at his kitchen table. He patiently shared his financial experience and personal time with me; I both remember and appreciate it to this day.

I'd also like to thank my proofreading team, Renee Staenglen, Linda Spencer, and Mike Curzio; who gave selflessly of their time and efforts to walk through the materials herein offering their perspective and suggestions so that more people can glean greater benefit from each of the worksheets. The book wouldn't be as effective working from my perspective alone and their help and input was invaluable.

INTRODUCTION

The purpose of this workbook is to give those who wish to take control of their personal finances a structured way to do so without having to spend the time to figure out how to organize the work themselves. Many of the ideas and activities discussed and contained herein are common knowledge as many people use similar methods and approaches to managing their finances. What I've attempted to do with this workbook is offer a structure that is easy to understand and use so that when it comes time to work with your finances, you can do so quickly, efficiently, and with as little effort as possible. If there's less work involved, you'll be more likely to get and stay involved and therefore accomplish more with your available finances.

The workbook has been organized on an annual basis, offering 12 monthly budget worksheets for use through the course of one year. Other monthly worksheets such as the Multiple Income Logs are similarly organized so that you can keep your annual financial records in one bound volume.

In teaching the many students that I have worked with over the years, I find many people don't work with budgets because they either don't know where to start, or they don't know how to organize the load of information that their financial activities generate. I hope that this volume provides you with a valuable shortcut to keeping your financial information organized in less complicated fashion so that you will have an easier time taking control of your income and expenses.

Once you understand what each worksheet and section does for you, you can approach your copy of the workbook with your financial idea or information, quickly locate the best place to deal with it, write it down, and go on with your day. When you do make time to work with your budget, your information will be organized in one convenient bound volume where you can deal with it without losing track of details or having it get disorganized and confusing. Once you are familiar with the organization of the workbook, it can help you reduce the frustration of keeping track of your income, expenses, and financial goals so that you are less averse to working with and benefitting from your financial records and plans. There are few things more frustrating than having a creative or important idea slip from your grasp because you have to spend time preparing and organizing to work with it.

There are many financial self-help books out on the market, but many begin at a point where people already have a grasp on financial management tools and may already have money to work with, as with many investing books. This work was written to help those who think they don't have money, to help them accurately track the money that they have so that they can manage it and have more to work with. This volume is a precursor to those tomes that guide you through 'what to do with your money once you have some'. Once you have your expenses on paper and can see the flow of your money through income and expenses, you can more easily manage funds and guide them to where they can be most effective for you.

If your motivation for seeking financial information and help is to reduce or eliminate your debt load, I applaud you. The social climate of western civilizations since World War II have been progressively more prone to use debt for ever broadening reasons. Today, in difficult economic times, people are even using credit to supplement cash flow from income to support daily expenses like groceries and gasoline without targeting the same expenses to be paid off at the end of the month. So, if you've picked up this volume as a personal interest in getting your debts under control, take heart. Realizing there is a problem or a situation renders the matter half-solved.

At the time of this writing The United States and the world is mired in a brewing financial storm that has the building world-wide kinetic financial energy to make the Great Depression of the 1930's look like a hiccup. I hope that I can play a small part in empowering people everywhere by helping them better utilize their own money and growing wealth to be less dependent upon easy access to credit which can cost them more money every time they use it. Imagine what the financial state of nations around the world would be if citizens had several years of income in the bank, in investments, and in retirement funds. The capital shortages that are slowing the economy currently would be less of an issue as people everywhere would have their own capital to call upon and banks and credit unions would have capital on deposit to loan for financing purposes. The economy would be strengthened; people around the world would be both empowered and encouraged. The growing and persistent uncertainty yielding a pervading lack of encouragement gleaned from the actions of our separate and respective governments, however, is an issue for another book by another author.

While it takes time to accomplish the grand goal of creating your own reserve of money; your own wealth, the time to begin that process is now. If you can't see that goal right now because you're at the bottom of a significant hole with many outstanding debts, don't worry; every problem has a solution. That doesn't mean the solution for your situation will be easy or painless, but there are solutions. A good financial advisor can help you outline plans to solve larger debt problems and the activities in this book will prepare you for a meaningful conversation with a professional money manager to those ends. Whether your situation will require you to move mountains or eat the proverbial elephant, keep your focus on the next rock that needs moved or the next bite and not the whole problem. One step at a time will get you there.

Whatever your present financial state, take control of your situation and look forward to goals that you will set for yourself. I hope that this volume is key in assisting you to both manage your finances and move toward your personal financial goals. Best wishes.

FORWARD

The sections of the workbook are each linked to the central form, the **Monthly Budget** Worksheet. This sheet is the cornerstone of your financial management program and you'll focus on its information and organization each month. Income and expenses are logged and managed here, but can be fed with information from the other worksheets which allow more detail and space to work with information than can be logged in the columns and rows of the Monthly Budget.

The Monthly **Cash Flow** Worksheet (Ch. 1), which encourages you to analyze your spending habits, is an exercise that helps you manage that activity. With it you will log all your expenses and see where your money is going, and in what form you tend to pay for things. This activity is echoed in the **Monthly Budget** Worksheet (Ch. 2) as the section labeled Miscellaneous Expenses. You can view this as an abbreviated version of the Monthly Cash Flow Worksheet. Here you can track your petty cash or pocket money monthly and keep an eye on how much money you are spending and where that money is going. There are even two blank areas that you can use to categorize the information with a form of payment and expense category similar to the Monthly Cash Flow Worksheet if you choose.

The **Financial Goal** Worksheet (Ch. 3) also ties to the Monthly Budget Worksheet in that it

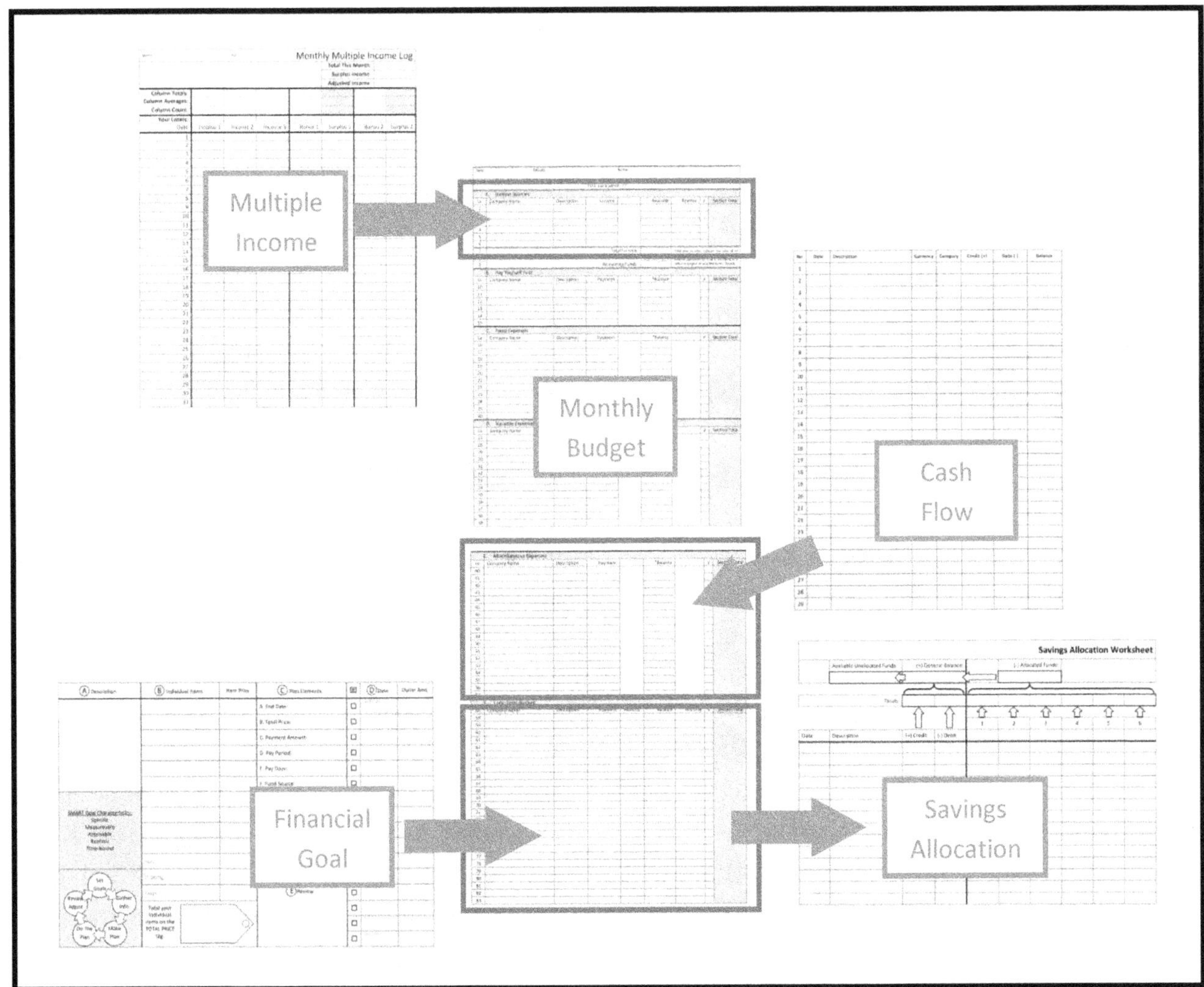

allows you to plan long-term goals that may have many parts to be considered, as with a vacation with many expenses and an extended time to plan for them. Once you figure the specifics of your long-term goal on the Financial Goal Worksheet, it's key parts can be entered into your Monthly Budget Worksheet in the Long-Term Budget section in the Payment, Months, and Monthly expense columns.

The **Savings Allocation** section (Ch. 6) also connects with the Long-Term Budget section of the Monthly Budget Worksheet. As you collect funds for your long-term goals and make deposits to one savings account, this worksheet will allow you to keep money in one account while tracking the individual purposes for which you are saving.

Finally, the **Multiple Income Monthly Log** (Ch. 4) allows you to track in greater detail incomes from several different sources. If you have more than one job, a business, or investments creating several streams of income, you can use these worksheets to track how this income is acquired and affects your overall budget. This sheet was originally written for a student who, working as a waitress and earning tips, told me in frustration that she couldn't run on a budget because she was never certain of how much money she would have available. The sheet organizes incomes and helps identify averages and surpluses so that you can operate financially on your average incomes and bank or stockpile your surpluses so that they are available when money is tight.

Not everyone will need to make use of the multiple income logs when starting out, but hopefully, using the materials here will allow you to identify money in your budget that you can set aside for personal financial goals. Once you have generated a stockpile of your own money you can plan to make investments, buy rental property, or start a business that each generate an additional income stream for yourself and your family. The bigger your ball of money, the better investment games you get to play. Just like carrying all your eggs in one basket, netting all your income from just one source isn't the most secure financial situation.

For those in debt, your first steps in this process will be some of your most important steps. The Monthly Cash Flow Worksheet (Ch. 1) will help you identify where your money comes from and goes to. Don't skip this exercise in the first section as it will help you analyze your habits in handling money; for ensuring good financial habits will determine your success. Also the Monthly Budget Worksheet will be of great assistance as it can help you target the most effective way to use the money that you have. Those first two chapters will be your cornerstones. Start small and you'll find that as one debt goes away you'll have more money to work on the next debt. The Monthly Budget can help you find opportunities to make that happen.

Finally, there are plans to make electronic versions of the worksheets available online that will automatically calculate all the math and results from the information that you enter into the form. These will offer the least time-consuming method for working with your financial information as the time you'd spend with a calculator is pre-programmed into the form and is calculated automatically. At the time of this writing, the website and its resources are under development.

Making the charts available online will give the greatest flexibility in that you don't have to be on your personal computer where specific software is installed. You will be able to log on through any computer or mobile device that has internet access, navigate to the mymoneysmart.com website, log into your account, and manage your records from almost anywhere. While in the planning stages at the time of this writing, we hope they will be a cornerstone to your future success.

Additional charts and graphs are also under development that can help you further analyze your financial information. Connecting to the information entered into each of the worksheets, the graphs will offer a visual representation of the information you are collecting. Often seeing the effects is much easier than interpreting a page full of numbers. The charts and graphs that are planned for online content, once available, will generate automatically from the information you provide in the forms.

I've felt that in light of current economic turmoil of 2011, that getting these resources into physical print would reach and help the largest number of people as not everybody who could benefit from this information has access to a computer and internet access. Efforts will continue to bring the online content to fruition as resources and personnel become available.

Please feel free to contact me and the staff with whom I hope to expand this effort with suggestions and requests to those ends.

DISCLAIMER

Neither MyMoneySmart.com, Do Something Smart With Your Money publications, nor their author and President David Pandone, nor any employees or representatives of our companies can promise or guarantee any degree of success from this publication, related seminars, website resources, or the information contained or presented herein. The companies, publications, officers, and author will not be held responsible for financial situations that result from exposure to or use of the information presented here in print, on our websites, or during related public or private seminars. While it is our collective intention to assist you with the information and topics of personal money management, we can only prepare and present the information. Any purchase or use of information in the published materials or presented in person is at the sole discretion of the attendee or reader and is undertaken at their own risk. Both patrons of our publications and attendees of our seminars are encouraged to seek the assistance and guidance of a professional financial advisor for help in determining strategies to implement for their specific financial circumstances and personal risk tolerance.

THE MONTHLY CASH FLOW WORKSHEET

1

As mentioned in the Forward section, the purpose of this book and I assume your purchase of it, is to help you gain control over your personal financial situation. Do bear in mind that each person's finances are a highly personal and private matter, often connected to some very important and emotionally charged topics. Before we can address a financial plan, situation, or problem, lets first discuss a few realities.

First, we must realize that any plan, situation, or problem that has arisen in your financial life is a result of the habits that you use in managing your finances. No plan, product, rule of law, or amount of money will ever *permanently* solve a financial problem created by a set of poorly chosen habits if the habits continue throughout and beyond the 'solution'. Hitting the lottery for millions while poor financial habits are still in use, is just more fuel for a bigger fire. If bad financial habits got you into a poor situation, only swapping those bad habits for good ones will get you out and keep you out of financial trouble permanently.

The truth is that people tend to live up to the extent of their financial capacity, buying nicer homes, nicer cars, nicer goodies, right up to the limit of what their finances can manage to float. We tend to live on that financial edge because an alarming number of us are not taught better strategies and are not infused with the motivation to do otherwise. If you don't learn good financial habits at home from family, financial success habits aren't taught in standard math classes in school and many of us simply miss them or must learn them the hard way. Metaphorically, the habits that can get you into one debt hole that you can't get out of without help, can get you right back into another debt hole. The second hole, however, can be both larger in width and depth than the hole you started in due to the false security of having more money with which to start. **Truth one:** Your habits will determine your success.

Second, you must be prepared to be honest with yourself or no person or plan can help you long-term in improving your financial situation. To address any problem, you must first identify that there is a problem, then set about accurately defining what that problem is. Only when you understand what the problem is and where it comes from can you begin to implement effective solutions. In this chapter you are given the opportunity to discover for yourself if there are problems with the financial habits that you've been using. No one will look at your results unless you allow them to, and no one will tell you what you should or should not do with your money unless you ask them for their opinion or advise. You should, however, commit to or promise yourself that you will be accurate about the information that you collect here, so that you can deal with it effectively. My father would say, 'Thou shalt not kid thyself'. **Truth two:** Misleading yourself only takes you in a direction you don't want to go.

The Purpose of This Exercise:

You need look no farther than TV commercials with debt reduction companies, consolidation loans, bankruptcy lawyers, and business 'opportunities' clogging the many commercial breaks to see that there are many people willing to 'help' you. Not to say that none of these options are a viable part of a solution, because they can be, but until you commit to changing your financial habits they can only be a temporary solution and will likely lead you back into a larger more frustrating situation than you may be in currently.

Before we get into the meat and potatoes of developing a personal budget, we first need to take a look at your personal money management habits. The ledger included in this first chapter is very much like a savings or checkbook ledger, only instead of tracking one bank account, you'll track yourself as a pass-through for all of your finances. I assume you have a source of income like a job and that you spend your income on a variety of monthly expenses. Using the Cash Flow Worksheet you'll track your income and expenses as well as the category of the expense and the currency type that you use to pay for each item. Tracking these aspects can give you valuable insight into your personal financial habits.

Tracking yourself as a pass-through for all your finances, you must consider that if you receive money from your job, or any other source, you have net income. You also have income if you take money from a savings account, 401K, investment account, or other source that may belong to you or be under your control. By setting savings or retirement money aside, you assigned it to a different purpose other than your personal budget. Withdrawing it places it back into your personal budget and back under your direct control. Bear in mind, although it is your money, what you're trying to track with this activity is the movement of money through you, so enter into the ledger any money that you have direct control over when you either receive it or spend it. Knowing where the money is coming from and where it is going to will allow you to 'see it', and thereby gain control over it.

There's no need to enter **current balances** for your other accounts such as savings or retirement, but make entries for the money added to or taken from those accounts as it moves through you. In other words, note the money you divert from your paycheck to deposit to these accounts, and note any withdrawal from those accounts, thereby tracking where money under your control came from and where it has gone.

Let's Get Started:

I recommend that you complete the Monthly Cash Flow Worksheet activity *prior to* attending a financial seminar or seeking the help of a financial advisor. The information that you'll gather will be highly valuable in how effectively someone can help you or in how effectively you'll be able to help yourself. No one assisting you will need to see the results, but what you'll learn about your habits from the exercise will provide priceless information in the financial planning process.

Do not change your current financial habits in anticipation of making your results look good or making yourself feel better. You're not trying to impress anyone through this activity. You need accurate information on what your current habits **are** with money, not what they should be, so just track what you do. Don't worry about it, just write it down. Changes and possible improvements can be discussed and considered later once you have an accurate picture of your financial habits. If you are like most people I've worked with, however, even writing down the reality of the situation carries with it the inspiration for some degree of change.

I recommend that you track this information for at least 4 weeks and consider continuing to collect your personal financial information for up to 3 months. That amount of time will give you a good look at your financial habits and allow you to make more informed decisions. To save some time, you may enter information from memory going back to last week or last month, or as far back as your memory will serve you accurately. Remember, be honest with yourself. If you're at all in doubt, it would be wise to start from where you can log accurate information.

- ☐ Select a start date and an end date (1-3 months)
- ☐ Write down your end date and post it where you'll see it.
- ☐ Gather your information:
  - Collect register receipts
  - Set aside bank and credit statements
  - Tear out the worksheet, carry it with you, and log financial events as they occur.
- ☐ Categorize your information:
  - Enter a category for each expense
  - Enter the currency type for each expense
- ☐ Analyze your data:
  - Add and total the entries for each category
  - Add and total the entries for each currency
  - Enter the totals for each on the Cash Flow Totals Worksheet
  - As an option, breaking down the information by month can also provide additional information as category totals change month to month

Once you have totals for the sections you can compare the amounts of money that you spend for each purpose. This can give you insights into where your money goes. You can also learn much (and possibly more) about the type of currency you use when you make a purchase. Consider that using credit, a type of currency that uses other people's money for which they expect to be repaid with interest, costs you more than using cash or a debit card; both of which are your own money.

No	Date	Description	Currency	Category	Credit (+)	Debit (-)	Balance
1	12/12	Employer Paycheck	Deposit	Income	1250.00		1250.00
2	12/15	Lunch	Cash	Cash		7.50	1242.50
3	12/16	Mydis (auto brakes)	Credit	Auto		495.00	747.50
4	12/16	Groceries	Debit	Food		275.00	472.50
5	12/17	Chiropractor	Credit	Health		55.00	417.50
6	12/20	Christmas Shopping	Debit	Special		375.00	42.50
7	12/21	Dinner	Cash	Food		37.50	5.00
8	12/22	Fleet of Foot (running shoes)	Credit	Clothing		65.00	-60.00
9	12/27	Employer Paycheck	Deposit	Income	1250.00		1190.00
10	12/31	Taxi (out and back)	Cash	Auto		70.00	1120.00
11	1/1	Savings	Debit	PYF		200.00	920.00
12	1/1	Investment	Debit	PYF		300.00	620.00
13	1/1	Home Mortgage	Debit	Housing		575.00	45.00
14	1/1	Home Owners Association Dues	Debit	Housing		150.00	-105.00
15	1/1	Home Phone	Debit	Housing		46.00	-151.00
16	1/1	Cell Phone	Debit	Housing		70.00	-221.00
17	1/1	Electrical Utility	Debit	Housing		65.00	-286.00
18	1/1	Internet Access	Debit	Housing		45.00	-331.00

Currency – The form of payment you made or the form of payment made to you. The four forms suggested for use on this paper worksheet are as follows:

- ☐ **Cash** – usually currency that you have on hand, in pocket
- ☐ **Debit** – currency credit pulled from your bank account against your current balance
- ☐ **Credit** – money that does not belong to you, but that you choose to use for payment of your debt in exchange for goods or services, and will need to repay back to the creditor (credit card issuer, store credit, etc…) at a later date, along with additional money added as interest
- ☐ **Deposit** – positive credit issued to, or money added to your account from a source such as an employer

Category – the kind of expense that you've spent your money on. Tracking the general purpose for which you've spent and continue to spend money can sometimes help you identify areas of absolute 'need' and areas which you can easily target for a reduction in expenses. The general categories suggested for use with this exercise are:

- ☐ **Income** – money you receive from a paycheck, investment, or a gift
- ☐ **PYF** – Pay Yourself First, money that you save or invest for a specific purpose
- ☐ **Cash** – money in the form of currency that you carry with you for minor expenses
- ☐ **Housing** – expenses for keeping a roof over your head (rent, mortgage, HOA fees, repairs)
- ☐ **Food** – money spent putting food in the refrigerator, lunch, snacking, etc.
- ☐ **Transport** – anything you've spent getting you, your family, and your stuff from one place to another, including car payments, gasoline, upkeep, repairs, insurance, cab fare, plane tickets, etc.
- ☐ **Utility** – electric, water, gas, oil, coal, phone, cell phone, cable, internet, etc.
- ☐ **Child** – day care, school tuition, school supplies, school fees, allowance, etc.
- ☐ **Clothing** – for you, family, or friends, if you bought it to wear it, label it accordingly
- ☐ **Health** – doctors, dentists, chiropractors, vitamins, classes, books, running shoes, etc.
- ☐ **ProSrv** – professional services like tax preparation, accounting, legal counsel, etc.
- ☐ **Special** – Christmas shopping, birthday presents; and other things that don't happen monthly, but you do spend your money on them when they do come around

No	Date	Description	Currency	Category	Credit (+)	Debit (-)	Balance
1							
2							
3							
4							
5							
6							
7							
8							
9							
10							
11							
12							
13							
14							
15							
16							
17							
18							
19							
20							
21							
22							
23							
24							
25							
26							
27							
28							
29							

No	Date	Description	Currency	Category	Credit (+)	Debit (-)	Balance
1							
2							
3							
4							
5							
6							
7							
8							
9							
10							
11							
12							
13							
14							
15							
16							
17							
18							
19							
20							
21							
22							
23							
24							
25							
26							
27							
28							
29							

No	Date	Description	Currency	Category	Credit (+)	Debit (-)	Balance
1							
2							
3							
4							
5							
6							
7							
8							
9							
10							
11							
12							
13							
14							
15							
16							
17							
18							
19							
20							
21							
22							
23							
24							
25							
26							
27							
28							
29							

No	Date	Description	Currency	Category	Credit (+)	Debit (-)	Balance
1							
2							
3							
4							
5							
6							
7							
8							
9							
10							
11							
12							
13							
14							
15							
16							
17							
18							
19							
20							
21							
22							
23							
24							
25							
26							
27							
28							
29							

No	Date	Description	Currency	Category	Credit (+)	Debit (-)	Balance
1							
2							
3							
4							
5							
6							
7							
8							
9							
10							
11							
12							
13							
14							
15							
16							
17							
18							
19							
20							
21							
22							
23							
24							
25							
26							
27							
28							
29							

No	Date	Description	Currency	Category	Credit (+)	Debit (-)	Balance
1							
2							
3							
4							
5							
6							
7							
8							
9							
10							
11							
12							
13							
14							
15							
16							
17							
18							
19							
20							
21							
22							
23							
24							
25							
26							
27							
28							
29							

Monthly Cash Flow Totals

(Calculating monthly totals is optional)

Currency	Month 1	Month 2	Month 3	Total
Cash				
Debit				
Credit				
Deposit				

Category	Month 1	Month 2	Month 3	Total
Income				
PYF				
Cash				
Housing				
Food				
Transport				
Utility				
Child				
Clothing				
Health				
ProSrv				
Special				

THE MONTHLY BUDGET WORKSHEET

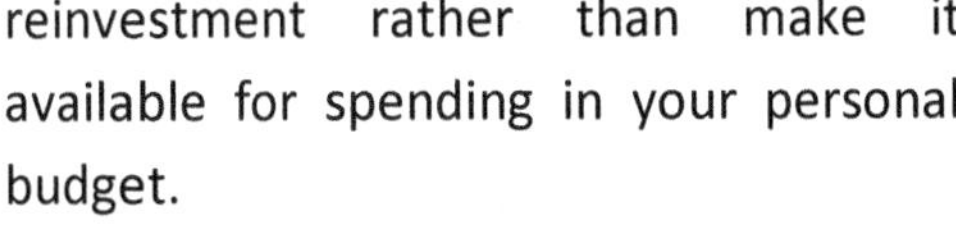

The Monthly Budget Worksheet has been designed to segment your income and expenses into general categories; each category sharing characteristics for how the money is collected or spent. Online resources which can calculate the results of your financial activity for you and display results in automatically generated charts and graphs will soon be available at mymoneysmart.com. Do visit us and look for these resources which are currently under development.

[+] The **Income Sources** (lines 1-6) section allows you to track several sources of money that come into your personal budget, along with money held in **reserve** for each source. If money is received from sources such as rental property or portfolio income like dividend yielding stocks, you may wish to record how much money is available, yet reserve all or part of that income in a separate account dedicated to that asset for expenses or reinvestment rather than make it available for spending in your personal budget.

The section has a **Section Total** area to the far right to total all your income (sum of **Income** column lines 1-6), and a space below the section on line 7 for **Total Income** that you choose to make available for expenses in your budget. As an accuracy check, the sum of all values in the **Available** and **Reserve** columns should also equal the **Section Total** amount to the far right. For multiple income sources, it can be beneficial to see all the funds available, even if you don't intend to use them in your budget, so that you can adjust where funds are allocated in the event that you run short or have excess funds available to be put to work elsewhere.

Below the Income Sources section are **lines 7-9** that sum up the activity on this worksheet: **Total Income** (that which you've made available

Year	Month	Name
2011	December	Julie Smith

Hint: Use a pencil... ☺

A. Income Sources

Ln	Company Name	Description	Income		Available	Reserve	√	Section Total
1	Julie's Café	12/12 Paycheck	1250.00		1250.00			**Sum Income (1-6)**
2	Bulls & Bears	Qtr Dividend	75.50		0.00	75.50		
3	Julie's Café	12/27 Paycheck	1250.00		1250.00			2925.50
4	Jenny's Party	Catering	350.00		225.00	125.00		
5								
6								**A**
7			Total Income (+):		2725.00	Total your income, subtract the total of all expenses on the worksheet, and adjust expense payments (D, E, & F) according to a deficit or surplus of available funds. Repeat.		
8			Total Expenses (-):		2685.55			
9			**Balance:**		39.45			

B. Pay Yourself First

Ln	Company Name	Description	Payment		Balance*		√	Section Total
10	North Central Bank	Savings	200.00		2525.00			**Sum PYF (10-15)**
11	Bulls & Bears	Investments	300.00		2225.00			
12								

for use in your budget), **Total Expenses** (the sum total of the expense sections in your monthly budget), and **Balance** (the *surplus* that you haven't allocated to some other purpose or *deficit* or shortfall amount that you haven't resolved). A balanced budget equates to zero when all is said and done. To those ends you should enter everything into your budget, even your pocket money, so that you can track where it's going. As you can see from the above example, Julie has nearly $40 that could be put to work elsewhere.

If your budget comes up short (a deficit, more expenses than income), line 9 will be a negative number. You'll need to reconsider how much money you've assigned to miscellaneous or variable expenses so that you'll have enough money to cover what absolutely must be covered. You can also reconsider income you marked as reserve on lines 1-6 and enter it into your budget, or consider deducting money from long-term goals so that you can meet your required expenses.

If you end up with a surplus (money left over) you can assign more money to savings, paying down debt, or spending money that you can enjoy and won't have to wonder about or feel guilty about keeping. You will have done the work in your budget to earn it and know that it doesn't belong somewhere else. If you write down everything, including pocket money, money left over should be viewed as money 'not working' or without purpose. Seek places that surplus funds can be effective in your budget and recalculate your numbers. Allocating more money for retirement, debt reduction, or buying more ice cream for your kids resulting in happier kids are all effective uses, but in different ways. Forty bucks buys a good amount of ice cream; but don't tell the kids, it's a surprise!

[-] The **Pay Yourself First** section (lines 10-15) is to track money that you set aside for savings and investment. If you spend everything you earn in one form or another, you aren't keeping any of the money you worked for and are not generating your own money; your own wealth. Some of your money should be set aside for retirement, for investment to grow your financial resources, and to cover expenses in an emergency so that you don't have to borrow or finance everything (which costs you more money). I've had people tell me they don't have money to invest or save. The reason you take the time and effort to do a budget is so that you can manage where your money is going to (and coming from) so that you can make decisions that result in more money being available for yourself. It is, after all, your money that you are working for. You should consider keeping some of it. If you don't have much money to spare, start small, but *start* a savings account. Develop the habit of saving, it's one of the key habits that generate wealth and will also boost your credit score over time.

[-] **Fixed Expenses** (lines 16-26) are bills that are the same all the time and don't change from month to month. These expenses can't easily be adjusted up or down just because you want to change them! The details of an installment loan, like a car payment, are all calculated when the loan is generated including the 'term' (duration) and all the payments are the same size; period. These payments simply can't be changed without doing something drastic like refinancing the house or trading in the car.

[-] **Variable Expenses** (lines 27-39) are those expenses that change each month depending on how much we use them. Some cell phone plans, utilities like electricity, groceries, health care, and credit card debt all fluctuate and depend on our consumption of the goods or services with which they are connected. The more or less we use the more or less we pay. This section is key to managing and keeping expenses within your

budget as you can adjust the expenses by adjusting your habits of consumption.

[-] **Miscellaneous Expenses** (lines 40-57) give money managers using these budgeting tools a place to track petty cash and other expenses. You can look at this section as pocket money or household petty cash and fund it with a set amount each month while tracking exactly where this money is going. By keeping records and reviewing these expenses, you may find that you could either use a bit more cash, or that you don't in fact spend all the cash you allowed yourself and can afford to shift some funds to another important purpose. Writing it down gives you a chance to look at it and make an informed decision.

If you completed the Monthly Cash Flow exercise from chapter 1, this section is a related carry-over exercise. An easy way to handle this information is to keep receipts from expenses and purchases throughout the month and log them when you do your budget. On every cash register receipt is the total expense and the method of payment. There are two blank columns that can be used to track the kind of payment that was used for each purchase. As with the Monthly Cash Flow exercise, often the type of payment (cash, credit, debit card, etc) is a key issue in controlling expenses.

[-] The **Long-Term Budget** section (lines 58-83) is used to track expenses that are not usually billed on a monthly basis and can sneak up on us if we don't have a way to organize them. For example, my car insurance premium or bill comes due every six months and the insurance company offers several ways to pay for it. You can pay it all in a lump sum, or split it into several payments *for an additional fee*. It's those service fees to split payments that will nickel and dime you to death if you don't take control of them. In the Long-Term Budget section you can set an amount of money aside each month so that when the bill comes due, you already have the money and can pay the bill without having to charge it or pay service fees. The Financial Goal Worksheet in chapter 3 is a good way to calculate a total cost and monthly costs for setting money aside for long-term purposes and more complex goals.

If your budget is tight, track this information in spite of not having the funds to cover it completely and pay what you can afford into a long-term fund or savings account. When the bill comes you can pay at least part of it with your own money and can lower your costs of financing that expense. It might take you several cycles on that bill to completely cover it with your own money, but the benefit of eliminating fees and interest for expenses totaling hundreds or thousands of dollars a year is worth it in the long run.

Some of the expenses you might consider for your long term section could include insurance premiums, auto maintenance like tires, oil changes, and regular service, down payments on new vehicles, medical expenses like orthodontics, and college tuition and expenses. You can really

F. Long Term Budget

Ln	Company Name	Description	Payment	Months	Balance*	Monthly	√	Section Total
58	Ensure Insurance	Premium	750.00	6		125.00		**Sum LTB Items (58-83)**
59	(Misc)	Auto Maint.	600.00	12		50.00		
60	New Car	Down-payment	3500.00	24		145.83		
61	Bulls & Bears	College-Missy	10,000.00	216		46.30		896.30
62	Bulls & Bears	College-Johnny	10,000.00	180		55.56		
63	Let's Go! Travel, Inc.	Disney Vacation	3500.00	18		194.44		
64	San Francisco Weekend	Vacation	1850.00	12		154.17		
65	Annual Shopping Spree	My Birthday!	1500.00	12		125.00		

save a lot of money by planning ahead over a number of years for expenses like these.

In the **Payment** section of the Long-Term Budget, enter the total lump-sum payment that you will need to spend for your long-term expense. In the **Months** column enter the number of months in the billing cycle, or number of months until the bill is due again. Divide the number of months into the payment and enter the figure in the **Monthly** column to break the expense down to a monthly payment. Finally, total all the expenses in the monthly column and enter the total in the Section Total at the far right; plan to divert these funds to another account.

I recommend using a savings account to collect the funds for the Long-Term section of the budget. You'll want these funds separate from funds you access regularly for paying bills and other expenses. Having these funds in a savings account will keep them accessible, but not so easily that they get spent 'by accident'. While interest rates are currently at multi-decade lows, your money can also earn a bit of interest while being collected for its long-term use. Even a little interest is nice to give yourself as a built-in discount. Chapter 6, the Savings Allocation Worksheet, introduces a chart that you can use to monitor and keep track of several purposes for intermingled funds in one account. One big ball of money with a way to track how much you have set aside for each purpose.

As mentioned earlier, online versions of this worksheet are under development at mymoneysmart.com that make not only the math, but adjustments to your budget easier as changes will be automatically calculated and the effect on your budget can be seen immediately. In the meantime, if you're working on paper:

1. Total your income (line 7 & block A)
2. Log all expenses, accurately
3. Add your expenses and total (line 8)
4. Subtract expenses from income (7 – 8 = ?)
5. Enter 7 vs. 8 difference (line 9) as balance
6. If the number is negative, find opportunities to cut back (sections D, E, & F) by the amount you are short on line 9
7. If the number is positive, find opportunities to save or invest (section B), pay down debt (section D), or reward yourself (section E).
8. Rerun steps 3- 5 to check balance.

Managing a budget on paper or in electronic form allows you to see income and expenses so that they can be managed. Like dials on a machine, you can dial up and down the funds allocated for each purpose to get the maximum benefit from your available resources and planning. The dials won't work if you don't know they're there or can't find them easily. Taking the time and spending the energy to write it all down and track it gives you the control you need over income and expenses to accomplish the things you need and want with your financial resources.

Year	Month	Name
	Hint: Use a pencil... ☺	

A. Income Sources

Ln	Company Name	Description	Income		Available	Reserve	√	Section Total
1								Sum Income (1-6)
2								
3								
4								
5								
6								A
7			Total Income (+):			Total your income, subtract the total of all expenses on the worksheet, and adjust expense payments (D, E, & F) according to a deficit or surplus of available funds. Repeat.		
8			Total Expenses (-):					
9			**Balance:**					

B. Pay Yourself First

Ln	Company Name	Description	Payment		Balance*		√	Section Total
10								Sum PYF (10-15)
11								
12								
13								
14								
15								B

C. Fixed Expenses

Ln	Company Name	Description	Payment		Balance*		√	Section Total
16								Sum Expenses (16-26)
17								
18								
19								
20								
21								
22								
23								
24								
25								
26								C

D. Variable Expenses

Ln	Company Name	Description	Payment		Balance*		√	Section Total
27								Sum Expenses (27-39)
28								
29								
30								
31								
32								
33								
34								
35								
36								
37								
38								
39								D

E. Miscellaneous Expenses

Ln	Company Name	Description	Payment		Balance*		√	Section Total
40								Sum Expenses (40-57)
41								
42								
43								
44								
45								
46								
47								
48								
49								
50								
51								
52								
53								
54								
55								
56								
57								**E**

F. Long Term Budget

Ln	Company Name	Description	Payment	Months	Balance*	Monthly	√	Section Total
58								Sum LTB Items (58-83)
59								
60								
61								
62								
63								
64								
65								
66								
67								
68								
69								
70								
71								
72								
73								
74								
75								
76								
77								
78								
79								
80								
81								
82								
83								**F**

*The balance column in the print version is optional

Year	Month	Name

Hint: Use a pencil... ☺

A. Income Sources

Ln	Company Name	Description	Income		Available	Reserve	√	Section Total
1								**Sum Income (1-6)**
2								
3								
4								
5								
6								**A**

Ln			
7	Total Income (+):		Total your income, subtract the total of all expenses on the worksheet, and adjust expense payments (D, E, & F) according to a deficit or surplus of available funds. Repeat.
8	Total Expenses (-):		
9	**Balance:**		

B. Pay Yourself First

Ln	Company Name	Description	Payment		Balance*		√	Section Total
10								**Sum PYF (10-15)**
11								
12								
13								
14								
15								**B**

C. Fixed Expenses

Ln	Company Name	Description	Payment		Balance*		√	Section Total
16								**Sum Expenses (16-26)**
17								
18								
19								
20								
21								
22								
23								
24								
25								
26								**C**

D. Variable Expenses

Ln	Company Name	Description	Payment		Balance*		√	Section Total
27								**Sum Expenses (27-39)**
28								
29								
30								
31								
32								
33								
34								
35								
36								
37								
38								
39								**D**

E. Miscellaneous Expenses

Ln	Company Name	Description	Payment		Balance*		√	Section Total
40								**Sum Expenses (40-57)**
41								
42								
43								
44								
45								
46								
47								
48								
49								
50								
51								
52								
53								
54								
55								
56								**E**
57								

F. Long Term Budget

Ln	Company Name	Description	Payment	Months	Balance*	Monthly	√	Section Total
58								**Sum LTB Items (58-83)**
59								
60								
61								
62								
63								
64								
65								
66								
67								
68								
69								
70								
71								
72								
73								
74								
75								
76								
77								
78								
79								
80								
81								
82								**F**
83								

*The balance column in the print version is optional

Year	Month	Name

Hint: Use a pencil... ☺

A. Income Sources

Ln	Company Name	Description	Income		Available	Reserve	√	Section Total
1								**Sum Income (1-6)**
2								
3								
4								
5								
6								**A**

Ln			
7	Total Income (+):		Total your income, subtract the total of all expenses on the worksheet, and adjust expense payments (D, E, & F) according to a deficit or surplus of available funds. Repeat.
8	Total Expenses (-):		
9	**Balance:**		

B. Pay Yourself First

Ln	Company Name	Description	Payment		Balance*		√	Section Total
10								**Sum PYF (10-15)**
11								
12								
13								
14								
15								**B**

C. Fixed Expenses

Ln	Company Name	Description	Payment		Balance*		√	Section Total
16								**Sum Expenses (16-26)**
17								
18								
19								
20								
21								
22								
23								
24								
25								
26								**C**

D. Variable Expenses

Ln	Company Name	Description	Payment		Balance*		√	Section Total
27								**Sum Expenses (27-39)**
28								
29								
30								
31								
32								
33								
34								
35								
36								
37								
38								
39								**D**

E. Miscellaneous Expenses								
Ln	Company Name	Description	Payment		Balance*		√	Section Total
40								Sum Expenses (40-57)
41								
42								
43								
44								
45								
46								
47								
48								
49								
50								
51								
52								
53								
54								
55								
56								**E**
57								

F. Long Term Budget								
Ln	Company Name	Description	Payment	Months	Balance*	Monthly	√	Section Total
58								Sum LTB Items (58-83)
59								
60								
61								
62								
63								
64								
65								
66								
67								
68								
69								
70								
71								
72								
73								
74								
75								
76								
77								
78								
79								
80								
81								
82								**F**
83								

*The balance column in the print version is optional

Year Month Name

Hint: Use a pencil... ☺

A. Income Sources

Ln	Company Name	Description	Income		Available	Reserve	√	Section Total
1								Sum Income (1-6)
2								
3								
4								
5								
6								A

Ln			
7	Total Income (+):		Total your income, subtract the total of all expenses on the worksheet, and adjust expense payments (D, E, & F) according to a deficit or surplus of available funds. Repeat.
8	Total Expenses (-):		
9	**Balance:**		

B. Pay Yourself First

Ln	Company Name	Description	Payment		Balance*		√	Section Total
10								Sum PYF (10-15)
11								
12								
13								
14								
15								B

C. Fixed Expenses

Ln	Company Name	Description	Payment		Balance*		√	Section Total
16								Sum Expenses (16-26)
17								
18								
19								
20								
21								
22								
23								
24								
25								
26								C

D. Variable Expenses

Ln	Company Name	Description	Payment		Balance*		√	Section Total
27								Sum Expenses (27-39)
28								
29								
30								
31								
32								
33								
34								
35								
36								
37								
38								
39								D

E. Miscellaneous Expenses

Ln	Company Name	Description	Payment		Balance*		√	Section Total
40								**Sum Expenses (40-57)**
41								
42								
43								
44								
45								
46								
47								
48								
49								
50								
51								
52								
53								
54								
55								
56								**E**
57								

F. Long Term Budget

Ln	Company Name	Description	Payment	Months	Balance*	Monthly	√	Section Total
58								**Sum LTB Items (58-83)**
59								
60								
61								
62								
63								
64								
65								
66								
67								
68								
69								
70								
71								
72								
73								
74								
75								
76								
77								
78								
79								
80								
81								
82								**F**
83								

*The balance column in the print version is optional

Year	Month	Name

Hint: Use a pencil… ☺

A. Income Sources

Ln	Company Name	Description	Income		Available	Reserve	√	Section Total
1								**Sum Income (1-6)**
2								
3								
4								
5								
6								**A**

Ln			
7	Total Income (+):		Total your income, subtract the total of all expenses on the worksheet, and adjust expense payments (D, E, & F) according to a deficit or surplus of available funds. Repeat.
8	Total Expenses (-):		
9	**Balance:**		

B. Pay Yourself First

Ln	Company Name	Description	Payment		Balance*		√	Section Total
10								**Sum PYF (10-15)**
11								
12								
13								
14								
15								**B**

C. Fixed Expenses

Ln	Company Name	Description	Payment		Balance*		√	Section Total
16								**Sum Expenses (16-26)**
17								
18								
19								
20								
21								
22								
23								
24								
25								
26								**C**

D. Variable Expenses

Ln	Company Name	Description	Payment		Balance*		√	Section Total
27								**Sum Expenses (27-39)**
28								
29								
30								
31								
32								
33								
34								
35								
36								
37								
38								
39								**D**

E. Miscellaneous Expenses

Ln	Company Name	Description	Payment		Balance*		√	Section Total
40								Sum Expenses (40-57)
41								
42								
43								
44								
45								
46								
47								
48								
49								
50								
51								
52								
53								
54								
55								
56								E
57								

F. Long Term Budget

Ln	Company Name	Description	Payment	Months	Balance*	Monthly	√	Section Total
58								Sum LTB Items (58-83)
59								
60								
61								
62								
63								
64								
65								
66								
67								
68								
69								
70								
71								
72								
73								
74								
75								
76								
77								
78								
79								
80								
81								
82								F
83								

*The balance column in the print version is optional

Year	Month	Name

Hint: Use a pencil... ☺

A. Income Sources

Ln	Company Name	Description	Income		Available	Reserve	√	Section Total
1								**Sum Income (1-6)**
2								
3								
4								
5								
6								**A**

Ln		
7	Total Income (+):	
8	Total Expenses (-):	
9	**Balance:**	

Total your income, subtract the total of all expenses on the worksheet, and adjust expense payments (D, E, & F) according to a deficit or surplus of available funds. Repeat.

B. Pay Yourself First

Ln	Company Name	Description	Payment		Balance*		√	Section Total
10								**Sum PYF (10-15)**
11								
12								
13								
14								
15								**B**

C. Fixed Expenses

Ln	Company Name	Description	Payment		Balance*		√	Section Total
16								**Sum Expenses (16-26)**
17								
18								
19								
20								
21								
22								
23								
24								
25								
26								**C**

D. Variable Expenses

Ln	Company Name	Description	Payment		Balance*		√	Section Total
27								**Sum Expenses (27-39)**
28								
29								
30								
31								
32								
33								
34								
35								
36								
37								
38								
39								**D**

E. Miscellaneous Expenses

Ln	Company Name	Description	Payment		Balance*		√	Section Total
40								**Sum Expenses (40-57)**
41								
42								
43								
44								
45								
46								
47								
48								
49								
50								
51								
52								
53								
54								
55								
56								**E**
57								

F. Long Term Budget

Ln	Company Name	Description	Payment	Months	Balance*	Monthly	√	Section Total
58								**Sum LTB Items (58-83)**
59								
60								
61								
62								
63								
64								
65								
66								
67								
68								
69								
70								
71								
72								
73								
74								
75								
76								
77								
78								
79								
80								
81								
82								**F**
83								

*The balance column in the print version is optional

Year	Month	Name
	Hint: Use a pencil… ☺	

A. Income Sources

Ln	Company Name	Description	Income		Available	Reserve	√	Section Total
1								Sum Income (1-6)
2								
3								
4								
5								
6								A
7	Total Income (+):					Total your income, subtract the total of all expenses on the worksheet, and adjust expense payments (D, E, & F) according to a deficit or surplus of available funds. Repeat.		
8	Total Expenses (-):							
9	**Balance:**							

B. Pay Yourself First

Ln	Company Name	Description	Payment		Balance*		√	Section Total
10								Sum PYF (10-15)
11								
12								
13								
14								
15								B

C. Fixed Expenses

Ln	Company Name	Description	Payment		Balance*		√	Section Total
16								Sum Expenses (16-26)
17								
18								
19								
20								
21								
22								
23								
24								
25								
26								C

D. Variable Expenses

Ln	Company Name	Description	Payment		Balance*		√	Section Total
27								Sum Expenses (27-39)
28								
29								
30								
31								
32								
33								
34								
35								
36								
37								
38								
39								D

E. Miscellaneous Expenses

Ln	Company Name	Description	Payment		Balance*		√	Section Total
40								**Sum Expenses (40-57)**
41								
42								
43								
44								
45								
46								
47								
48								
49								
50								
51								
52								
53								
54								
55								
56								**E**
57								

F. Long Term Budget

Ln	Company Name	Description	Payment	Months	Balance*	Monthly	√	Section Total
58								**Sum LTB Items (58-83)**
59								
60								
61								
62								
63								
64								
65								
66								
67								
68								
69								
70								
71								
72								
73								
74								
75								
76								
77								
78								
79								
80								
81								
82								**F**
83								

*The balance column in the print version is optional

Year Month Name

Hint: Use a pencil… ☺

A. Income Sources

Ln	Company Name	Description	Income		Available	Reserve	√	Section Total
1								**Sum Income (1-6)**
2								
3								
4								
5								
6								**A**
7			Total Income (+):			Total your income, subtract the total of all expenses on the worksheet, and adjust expense payments (D, E, & F) according to a deficit or surplus of available funds. Repeat.		
8			Total Expenses (-):					
9			**Balance:**					

B. Pay Yourself First

Ln	Company Name	Description	Payment		Balance*		√	Section Total
10								**Sum PYF (10-15)**
11								
12								
13								
14								
15								**B**

C. Fixed Expenses

Ln	Company Name	Description	Payment		Balance*		√	Section Total
16								**Sum Expenses (16-26)**
17								
18								
19								
20								
21								
22								
23								
24								
25								
26								**C**

D. Variable Expenses

Ln	Company Name	Description	Payment		Balance*		√	Section Total
27								**Sum Expenses (27-39)**
28								
29								
30								
31								
32								
33								
34								
35								
36								
37								
38								
39								**D**

E. Miscellaneous Expenses								
Ln	Company Name	Description	Payment		Balance*		√	Section Total
40								**Sum Expenses (40-57)**
41								
42								
43								
44								
45								
46								
47								
48								
49								
50								
51								
52								
53								
54								
55								
56								**E**
57								

F. Long Term Budget								
Ln	Company Name	Description	Payment	Months	Balance*	Monthly	√	Section Total
58								**Sum LTB Items (58-83)**
59								
60								
61								
62								
63								
64								
65								
66								
67								
68								
69								
70								
71								
72								
73								
74								
75								
76								
77								
78								
79								
80								
81								
82								**F**
83								

*The balance column in the print version is optional

Year	Month	Name

Hint: Use a pencil... ☺

A. Income Sources

Ln	Company Name	Description	Income		Available	Reserve	√	Section Total
1								**Sum Income (1-6)**
2								
3								
4								
5								
6								**A**

Ln			
7	Total Income (+):		Total your income, subtract the total of all expenses on the worksheet, and adjust expense payments (D, E, & F) according to a deficit or surplus of available funds. Repeat.
8	Total Expenses (-):		
9	**Balance:**		

B. Pay Yourself First

Ln	Company Name	Description	Payment		Balance*		√	Section Total
10								**Sum PYF (10-15)**
11								
12								
13								
14								
15								**B**

C. Fixed Expenses

Ln	Company Name	Description	Payment		Balance*		√	Section Total
16								**Sum Expenses (16-26)**
17								
18								
19								
20								
21								
22								
23								
24								
25								
26								**C**

D. Variable Expenses

Ln	Company Name	Description	Payment		Balance*		√	Section Total
27								**Sum Expenses (27-39)**
28								
29								
30								
31								
32								
33								
34								
35								
36								
37								
38								
39								**D**

E. Miscellaneous Expenses								
Ln	Company Name	Description	Payment		Balance*		√	Section Total
40								Sum Expenses (40-57)
41								
42								
43								
44								
45								
46								
47								
48								
49								
50								
51								
52								
53								
54								
55								
56								
57								E

F. Long Term Budget								
Ln	Company Name	Description	Payment	Months	Balance*	Monthly	√	Section Total
58								Sum LTB Items (58-83)
59								
60								
61								
62								
63								
64								
65								
66								
67								
68								
69								
70								
71								
72								
73								
74								
75								
76								
77								
78								
79								
80								
81								
82								
83								F

*The balance column in the print version is optional

Year Month Name

Hint: Use a pencil… ☺

A. Income Sources

Ln	Company Name	Description	Income		Available	Reserve	√	Section Total
1								**Sum Income (1-6)**
2								
3								
4								
5								
6								**A**

Ln			
7	Total Income (+):		Total your income, subtract the total of all expenses on the worksheet, and adjust expense payments (D, E, & F) according to a deficit or surplus of available funds. Repeat.
8	Total Expenses (-):		
9	**Balance:**		

B. Pay Yourself First

Ln	Company Name	Description	Payment		Balance*		√	Section Total
10								**Sum PYF (10-15)**
11								
12								
13								
14								
15								**B**

C. Fixed Expenses

Ln	Company Name	Description	Payment		Balance*		√	Section Total
16								**Sum Expenses (16-26)**
17								
18								
19								
20								
21								
22								
23								
24								
25								
26								**C**

D. Variable Expenses

Ln	Company Name	Description	Payment		Balance*		√	Section Total
27								**Sum Expenses (27-39)**
28								
29								
30								
31								
32								
33								
34								
35								
36								
37								
38								
39								**D**

E. Miscellaneous Expenses

Ln	Company Name	Description	Payment		Balance*		√	Section Total
40								Sum Expenses (40-57)
41								
42								
43								
44								
45								
46								
47								
48								
49								
50								
51								
52								
53								
54								
55								
56								E
57								

F. Long Term Budget

Ln	Company Name	Description	Payment	Months	Balance*	Monthly	√	Section Total
58								Sum LTB Items (58-83)
59								
60								
61								
62								
63								
64								
65								
66								
67								
68								
69								
70								
71								
72								
73								
74								
75								
76								
77								
78								
79								
80								
81								
82								F
83								

*The balance column in the print version is optional

Year Month Name

Hint: Use a pencil... ☺

A. Income Sources

Ln	Company Name	Description	Income		Available	Reserve	√	Section Total
1								Sum Income (1-6)
2								
3								
4								
5								
6								A

Ln			
7	Total Income (+):		Total your income, subtract the total of all expenses on the worksheet, and adjust expense payments (D, E, & F) according to a deficit or surplus of available funds. Repeat.
8	Total Expenses (-):		
9	**Balance:**		

B. Pay Yourself First

Ln	Company Name	Description	Payment		Balance*		√	Section Total
10								Sum PYF (10-15)
11								
12								
13								
14								
15								B

C. Fixed Expenses

Ln	Company Name	Description	Payment		Balance*		√	Section Total
16								Sum Expenses (16-26)
17								
18								
19								
20								
21								
22								
23								
24								
25								
26								C

D. Variable Expenses

Ln	Company Name	Description	Payment		Balance*		√	Section Total
27								Sum Expenses (27-39)
28								
29								
30								
31								
32								
33								
34								
35								
36								
37								
38								
39								D

	E. Miscellaneous Expenses							
Ln	Company Name	Description	Payment		Balance*		√	Section Total
40								**Sum Expenses (40-57)**
41								
42								
43								
44								
45								
46								
47								
48								
49								
50								
51								
52								
53								
54								
55								
56								
57								**E**

	F. Long Term Budget							
Ln	Company Name	Description	Payment	Months	Balance*	Monthly	√	Section Total
58								**Sum LTB Items (58-83)**
59								
60								
61								
62								
63								
64								
65								
66								
67								
68								
69								
70								
71								
72								
73								
74								
75								
76								
77								
78								
79								
80								
81								
82								
83								**F**

*The balance column in the print version is optional

Year	Month	Name

Hint: Use a pencil… ☺

A. Income Sources

Ln	Company Name	Description	Income		Available	Reserve	√	Section Total
1								**Sum Income (1-6)**
2								
3								
4								
5								
6								**A**

Ln			
7	Total Income (+):		Total your income, subtract the total of all expenses on the worksheet, and adjust expense payments (D, E, & F) according to a deficit or surplus of available funds. Repeat.
8	Total Expenses (-):		
9	**Balance:**		

B. Pay Yourself First

Ln	Company Name	Description	Payment		Balance*		√	Section Total
10								**Sum PYF (10-15)**
11								
12								
13								
14								
15								**B**

C. Fixed Expenses

Ln	Company Name	Description	Payment		Balance*		√	Section Total
16								**Sum Expenses (16-26)**
17								
18								
19								
20								
21								
22								
23								
24								
25								
26								**C**

D. Variable Expenses

Ln	Company Name	Description	Payment		Balance*		√	Section Total
27								**Sum Expenses (27-39)**
28								
29								
30								
31								
32								
33								
34								
35								
36								
37								
38								
39								**D**

E. Miscellaneous Expenses

Ln	Company Name	Description	Payment		Balance*		√	Section Total
40								**Sum Expenses (40-57)**
41								
42								
43								
44								
45								
46								
47								
48								
49								
50								
51								
52								
53								
54								
55								
56								
57								**E**

F. Long Term Budget

Ln	Company Name	Description	Payment	Months	Balance*	Monthly	√	Section Total
58								**Sum LTB Items (58-83)**
59								
60								
61								
62								
63								
64								
65								
66								
67								
68								
69								
70								
71								
72								
73								
74								
75								
76								
77								
78								
79								
80								
81								
82								**F**
83								

*The balance column in the print version is optional

THE FINANCIAL GOAL WORKSHEET

The accompanying chart is predicated upon some common and basic principles for goal setting. Let's first establish exactly where you want to go, precisely what you want to accomplish, then formulate a plan that will take you there:

SMART Goal Characteristics:

Specific – If your goal is not specific enough, you will lack the information to accurately hit your target. For example, if your goal is a new car, leaving out of the planning stages the options packages, custom wheels, and sound system will leave you with much less money than it will actually take to buy the car as you see in your mind. Shortcutting the thoughtful consideration of your goal at this very important step will lead to problems later in the planning steps.

Measureable – For financial planning purposes, the goal you are setting takes money to achieve. Carefully considering all the components that make up that goal will give you the cost of each component, which when added together, will give you the total cost of your goal. *General* goals that lack specific details leave holes in your planning and place you off-target on your total price. Shortsighted trip planning might get you a week in Paris, but may leave you with no food to eat and no way to get there; or no way to get back home!

Attainable and Realistic – These components in our planning purposes are combined in the **C. Plan Elements** section of the chart. Since we are financial planning, the buttons and dials on this machine are pretty consistent. These buttons and dials are the elements discussed in the **Financial Planning Process** called **3. Make a Plan**. Producing honest and accurate answers to these questions which work with your personal financial resources makes the plan both attainable and realistic.

Time-bound – Goals without a target date, a deadline, aren't really goals; they're ideas, dreams, nice things to talk about over lunch... If you're serious about accomplishing the things you set out to do, you must set a realistic time frame in which you can put forth the efforts and gather the resources to do them. Carefully considering the details in the previous sections allows you to accurately target the size of the final **PRICE TAG** and measure, based on your personal resources, the amount of time needed to accumulate funds to cover that price tag. If you've planned carefully, there's only following through on what you planned, the 'just do it' factor, that stands between you and what you want.

The Financial Planning Process:

The financial planning Process includes the steps around which our Financial Goal Worksheet is written.

1. Set your Goal – be very specific about what you want in the **Description** section. A new cell phone

without accessories and the right apps won't be as useful or fun as you imagined. Whatever your goal, *everything* isn't always included, so include all the items you'll want along with your goal in your plan so you can plan to pay for them.

2. Gather Information – Working from your very specific description, list the Individual Items that when added together make up the goal that you have in mind. Spend some time looking for sources, vendors, and the best prices for these items. Note the cost of each of the items next to their description. Once you're certain you've included *everything*, add up the cost and enter it in the **TOTAL PRICE** tag at the bottom of the column. When you have the money to cover the PRICE TAG, you can go get your goal. It's not a bad idea to allow someone else to put their eyes on your list at this point. Their fresh perspective might see a few necessary things that belong on the list that you may have missed.

3. Make a Plan – Here we establish the **Plan Elements** that make your plan possible. Answer the following questions, not necessarily in order, and place the answers on your chart in the **C. Plan Elements** section:

A. **End Date:** When do you want to have your goal?
B. **Total Price:** What's the cash amount you'll need to buy these items? (restate your PRICE TAG)
C. **Payment Amount:** Dividing the **Total Price** by the number of **Pay Periods** (or months) gives you the amount you'll need to set aside each time.
D. **Pay Period:** How often are you paid?
E. **Pay Days:** How many **Pay Periods** occur between your **Start Date** and your **End Date** (the term)?
F. **Fund Source:** Will you pay for this goal from your paycheck, or from some other source of income? If it's not a steady paycheck, carefully consider on what dates you will receive this income.
G. **Start Date:** When will you have to start on this plan considering the resources that you have to apply to this goal? Refer to a calendar and count back in Pay Periods from your End Date.
H. **Affirmation:** Write one sentence containing all the elements above that encapsulates both your final goal and the steps for the plan you established to make that goal happen. For example: "I will by September 15, 2012, have accumulated $2450.00 by setting aside $98.00 from each of 25 paychecks beginning Sept. 1 2011 so that I can take a 7 day vacation to Key West Florida on December 18, 2012." Write it down on paper and post it where you'll see it and read it every day.

4. Act on or Do Your Plan – Divert the amount of money you calculated for each payment on dates that coincide with your paychecks, income, or cash flow. Enter the dates and payments in section 4. Each month when you work with your budget, or when you receive your paycheck, put the money aside, preferably in an interest bearing account so that you earn some interest while you're working toward your goal. If you do it, you'll have the money when you get to your End Date and you'll have your goal! You've planned your work, now work your plan.

5. Review and Adjust – If you're working your plan and things are not working as you intended, or new circumstances have presented themselves that are interfering with the plan, you may need to sit down and push the buttons and turn the dials on your goal machine again. List in section 5 the Plan Elements in section 4 that are causing problems with your plan. Consider adjustments to this plan or writing a new plan to work around these issues.

The **Plan Elements** established in step **3. Make a Plan** are control factors; the buttons and dials on your goal machine. The <u>term</u> (length of time to fulfill your goal), the <u>price tag</u> (total cost) and the <u>payment</u> (how much you set aside each pay period) are your main dials. Adjusting these factors significantly changes how your plan performs. If you end up with less money because your hours at work are cut back, or your spouse loses their job, you can move the start or end dates giving yourself more time. More time means making smaller but a higher number of payments. If you take another job or create a supplemental income source, you can shorten the term by increasing payment sizes, or changing the frequency because one job pays you on the week in between the other job. As your situation changes, consider whether your plan needs to change.

There is no one fixed answer to financial success, and no magic formula or spell that will 'allakhazam!' you to your goals. There's only the knowledge you can gain in learning how to build a financial machine, how to control that machine, and how to fix it when it coughs and sputters and doesn't run the way you hope it would. You can make your financial goals as simple or as complex as you like. I hope you enjoy the journey. Happy motoring!

(A) Description	(B) Individual Items	Item Price	(C) Plan Elements:	☒	(D) Date	Dollar Amt.
Weekend Trip to San Francisco For Concert & Pro-Football Game	Rental Car (4 days)	100.00	A. End Date: October 15, 2012	☐	Start Date:	
	Gasoline	150.00	B. Total Price: $1850.00	☐	Nov. 15	$154.17
	Weston Hotel (2 nights)	700.00	C. Payment Amount: $154.17	☐	Dec. 15	$154.17
	Dinner (2 nights)	300.00	D. Pay Period: 4 weeks	☐	Jan. 15	$154.17
	Lunch (2 days)	75.00	E. Pay Days: 12	☐	Feb. 15	$154.17
	Concert Tickets	150.00	F. Fund Source: Monthly Budget	☐	Mar. 15	$154.17
	Football Tickets	125.00	G. Start Date: October 15, 2011	☐	Apr. 15	$154.17
SMART Goal Characteristics: Specific, Measureable, Attainable, Realistic, Time-bound	Spending Money	250.00	H. Affirmation: "I will... by October 15, 2012, have saved $1850.00 by setting aside $154.17 each month from my monthly budget beginning October 15, 2011 so that we can take 3-day, 2-night trip to San Francisco for a concert and pro-football game."	☐	May 15	$154.17
				☐	Jun. 15	$154.17
				☐	Jul. 15	$154.17
	Fees			☐	Aug. 15	$154.17
	Shipping			☐	Sep. 15	$154.17
Set Goals → Gather Info → Make Plan → Do The Plan → Review Adjust	Taxes		(E) Review:	☐	Oct. 15	$154.17
	Total your individual items on the TOTAL PRICE tag:	$1850.00		☐		
				☐		
				☐	End Date:	

(A) Description	(B) Individual Items	Item Price	(C) Plan Elements:	☒	(D) Date	Dollar Amt.
			A. End Date:	☐	Start Date:	
			B. Total Price:	☐		
			C. Payment Amount:	☐		
			D. Pay Period:	☐		
			E. Pay Days:	☐		
			F. Fund Source:	☐		
			G. Start Date:	☐		
SMART Goal Characteristics: Specific Measureable Attainable Realistic Time-bound			H. Affirmation: "I will... "	☐		
				☐		
				☐		
	Fees			☐		
Set Goals Gather Info Make Plan Do The Plan Review Adjust	Shipping			☐		
	Taxes		(E) Review:	☐		
	Total your individual items on the TOTAL PRICE tag:			☐		
				☐		
				☐	End Date:	

(A) Description	(B) Individual Items	Item Price	(C) Plan Elements:	☒	(D) Date	Dollar Amt.
			A. End Date:	☐	Start Date:	
			B. Total Price:	☐		
			C. Payment Amount:	☐		
			D. Pay Period:	☐		
			E. Pay Days:	☐		
			F. Fund Source:	☐		
SMART Goal Characteristics: Specific Measureable Attainable Realistic Time-bound			G. Start Date:	☐		
			H. Affirmation: "I will...	☐		
				☐		
				☐		
	Fees			☐		
Set Goals Gather Info Make Plan Do The Plan Review Adjust	Shipping		"	☐		
	Taxes		(E) Review:	☐		
	Total your individual items on the TOTAL PRICE tag:			☐		
				☐		
				☐	End Date:	

(A) Description	(B) Individual Items	Item Price	(C) Plan Elements:	☒	(D) Date	Dollar Amt.
			A. End Date:	☐	Start Date:	
			B. Total Price:	☐		
			C. Payment Amount:	☐		
			D. Pay Period:	☐		
			E. Pay Days:	☐		
			F. Fund Source:	☐		
SMART Goal Characteristics: Specific Measureable Attainable Realistic Time-bound			G. Start Date:	☐		
			H. Affirmation: "I will… "	☐		
				☐		
				☐		
	Fees			☐		
Set Goals → Gather Info → Make Plan → Do The Plan → Review Adjust	Shipping			☐		
	Taxes		(E) Review:	☐		
	Total your individual items on the TOTAL PRICE tag:			☐		
				☐		
				☐	End Date:	

Ⓐ Description	Ⓑ Individual Items	Item Price	Ⓒ Plan Elements:	☒	Ⓓ Date	Dollar Amt.
			A. End Date:	☐	Start Date:	
			B. Total Price:	☐		
			C. Payment Amount:	☐		
			D. Pay Period:	☐		
			E. Pay Days:	☐		
			F. Fund Source:	☐		
SMART Goal Characteristics: Specific Measureable Attainable Realistic Time-bound			G. Start Date:	☐		
			H. Affirmation: "I will... "	☐		
				☐		
				☐		
	Fees			☐		
	Shipping			☐		
Set Goals → Gather Info → Make Plan → Do The Plan → Review Adjust	Taxes			☐		
	Total your individual items on the TOTAL PRICE tag:		Ⓔ Review:	☐		
				☐		
				☐	End Date:	

(A) Description	(B) Individual Items	Item Price	(C) Plan Elements:	☒	(D) Date	Dollar Amt.
			A. End Date:	☐	Start Date:	
			B. Total Price:	☐		
			C. Payment Amount:	☐		
			D. Pay Period:	☐		
			E. Pay Days:	☐		
			F. Fund Source:	☐		
SMART Goal Characteristics: Specific Measureable Attainable Realistic Time-bound			G. Start Date:	☐		
			H. Affirmation: "I will... "	☐		
				☐		
				☐		
	Fees			☐		
Set Goals → Gather Info → Make Plan → Do The Plan → Review Adjust	Shipping			☐		
	Taxes		(E) Review:	☐		
	Total your individual items on the TOTAL PRICE tag:			☐		
				☐		
				☐	End Date:	

Ⓐ Description	Ⓑ Individual Items	Item Price	Ⓒ Plan Elements:	☒	Ⓓ Date	Dollar Amt.
			A. End Date:	☐	Start Date:	
			B. Total Price:	☐		
			C. Payment Amount:	☐		
			D. Pay Period:	☐		
			E. Pay Days:	☐		
			F. Fund Source:	☐		
SMART Goal Characteristics: Specific Measureable Attainable Realistic Time-bound			G. Start Date:	☐		
			H. Affirmation: "I will... "	☐		
				☐		
				☐		
	Fees			☐		
Set Goals → Gather Info → Make Plan → Do The Plan → Review Adjust	Shipping			☐		
	Taxes		Ⓔ Review:	☐		
	Total your individual items on the TOTAL PRICE tag:			☐		
				☐		
				☐	End Date:	

(A) Description	(B) Individual Items	Item Price	(C) Plan Elements:	☒	(D) Date	Dollar Amt.
			A. End Date:	☐	Start Date:	
			B. Total Price:	☐		
			C. Payment Amount:	☐		
			D. Pay Period:	☐		
			E. Pay Days:	☐		
			F. Fund Source:	☐		
			G. Start Date:	☐		
SMART Goal Characteristics: Specific Measureable Attainable Realistic Time-bound			H. Affirmation: "I will...	☐		
				☐		
				☐		
	Fees			☐		
	Shipping		"	☐		
Set Goals Gather Info Make Plan Do The Plan Review Adjust	Taxes		(E) Review:	☐		
	Total your individual items on the TOTAL PRICE tag:			☐		
				☐		
				☐	End Date:	

(A) Description	(B) Individual Items	Item Price	(C) Plan Elements:	☒	(D) Date	Dollar Amt.
			A. End Date:	☐	Start Date:	
			B. Total Price:	☐		
			C. Payment Amount:	☐		
			D. Pay Period:	☐		
			E. Pay Days:	☐		
			F. Fund Source:	☐		
SMART Goal Characteristics: Specific Measureable Attainable Realistic Time-bound			G. Start Date:	☐		
			H. Affirmation: "I will... "	☐		
				☐		
				☐		
	Fees			☐		
Set Goals → Gather Info → Make Plan → Do The Plan → Review Adjust	Shipping			☐		
	Taxes		(E) Review:	☐		
	Total your individual items on the TOTAL PRICE tag:			☐		
				☐		
				☐	End Date:	

(A) Description	(B) Individual Items	Item Price	(C) Plan Elements:	☒	(D) Date	Dollar Amt.
			A. End Date:	☐	Start Date:	
			B. Total Price:	☐		
			C. Payment Amount:	☐		
			D. Pay Period:	☐		
			E. Pay Days:	☐		
			F. Fund Source:	☐		
SMART Goal Characteristics: Specific Measureable Attainable Realistic Time-bound			G. Start Date:	☐		
			H. Affirmation: "I will... "	☐		
				☐		
				☐		
	Fees			☐		
Set Goals → Gather Info → Make Plan → Do The Plan → Review Adjust	Shipping			☐		
	Taxes		(E) Review:	☐		
	Total your individual items on the TOTAL PRICE tag:			☐		
				☐		
				☐	End Date:	

(A) Description	(B) Individual Items	Item Price	(C) Plan Elements:	☒	(D) Date	Dollar Amt.
			A. End Date:	☐	Start Date:	
			B. Total Price:	☐		
			C. Payment Amount:	☐		
			D. Pay Period:	☐		
			E. Pay Days:	☐		
			F. Fund Source:	☐		
SMART Goal Characteristics: Specific Measureable Attainable Realistic Time-bound			G. Start Date:	☐		
			H. Affirmation: "I will... "	☐		
				☐		
				☐		
	Fees			☐		
Set Goals → Gather Info → Make Plan → Do The Plan → Review Adjust	Shipping			☐		
	Taxes		(E) Review:	☐		
	Total your individual items on the TOTAL PRICE tag:			☐		
				☐		
				☐	End Date:	

(A) Description	(B) Individual Items	Item Price	(C) Plan Elements:	☒	(D) Date	Dollar Amt.
			A. End Date:	☐	Start Date:	
			B. Total Price:	☐		
			C. Payment Amount:	☐		
			D. Pay Period:	☐		
			E. Pay Days:	☐		
			F. Fund Source:	☐		
SMART Goal Characteristics: Specific Measureable Attainable Realistic Time-bound			G. Start Date:	☐		
			H. Affirmation: "I will... "	☐		
				☐		
				☐		
	Fees			☐		
Set Goals → Gather Info → Make Plan → Do The Plan → Review Adjust	Shipping			☐		
	Taxes		(E) Review:	☐		
	Total your individual items on the TOTAL PRICE tag:			☐		
				☐		
				☐	End Date:	

(A) Description	(B) Individual Items	Item Price	(C) Plan Elements:	☒	(D) Date	Dollar Amt.
			A. End Date:	☐	Start Date:	
			B. Total Price:	☐		
			C. Payment Amount:	☐		
			D. Pay Period:	☐		
			E. Pay Days:	☐		
			F. Fund Source:	☐		
SMART Goal Characteristics: Specific Measureable Attainable Realistic Time-bound			G. Start Date:	☐		
			H. Affirmation: "I will... "	☐		
				☐		
				☐		
	Fees			☐		
Set Goals → Gather Info → Make Plan → Do The Plan → Review Adjust	Shipping			☐		
	Taxes		(E) Review:	☐		
	Total your individual items on the TOTAL PRICE tag:			☐		
				☐		
				☐	End Date:	

THE MULTIPLE INCOME MONTHLY LOG

4

The Multiple Income Log was designed to help those with several sources of income to organize and better plan for the productive use of their cash flow. Those whose income streams are intermittent and from varied sources, such as tips or consulting, can find budgeting challenging as income is inconsistent from month to month and may not be received at regular intervals.

The idea behind this solution is that when income is intermittent, income needs to be averaged over time and the resulting cash flow used within the confines of the *average* income. The worksheet helps you track income and calculate both the averages and surpluses; wages in excess of the average. We'll also need to resist the urge to expand our expenses to a larger lifestyle when times are 'good'. Next week or next month may not be as good and may not provide the resources to continue the expanded lifestyle. When times are good surplus cash flow can be 'saved for a rainy day'; a day when times may not be so good. To use it, we must first locate how much of it is actually surplus, or over and above our average income. So, an old idea for certain, but with a way to track and plan for it.

Using the Worksheet

The worksheet has 31 numbered rows for the days of the month and seven columns to organize five different income sources. **The first three columns** are used for regular, predictable forms of income. If used for one person with several personal income sources you can track them under **Income 1-3**. In these columns you may only have two entries each month if you are paid every other week; so, not every cell on the sheet needs to be filled. Couples, domestic partners, and room-mates might want to track income for each person or income source using one column for each person. Considering the entire household and calculating averages and percentages as a group all on one page may help organize an otherwise complex affair. Be sure to log the paycheck entry on the date the check was written to keep your records consistent.

The four columns on the right are to track the inconsistent income that might come from things like tips, bonuses, sales commissions (if you wish to track them separately) or even paychecks from inconsistent work hours. Intermittent income sources like cake decorating, house cleaning, tax preparation, and home improvements are examples of activities that some people do in addition to their job or occupation. These activities may not provide income at regular intervals, but to affectively budget this sporadic income you must track it. Log these income sources under the **Bonus 1 and Bonus 2** columns.

Whenever you get paid, log the income in the column you assigned to that income source on the line that corresponds to the date you received that money. Notice that a space has been left above the column headers for you to add your own short label. At the end of the month, which may coincide with when you pay your bills, you'll have all your numbers in view so that you can deal with them.

The first sheet has been filled out as an *example* for how to use the system. The data on the example represents the income of a waiter or waitress in the month of December. A waiter may make a low hourly wage and depend upon their tips for a good portion of their income, though tips can vary widely over weeks and months.

In the example, our waiter pulls in an hourly paycheck every week of $150. The income is logged on the sheet so that the entry matches the date on the paycheck. To calculate the top of the column, count the entries (4) and enter the number in the **Column Count** row. Add the entries and place the **sum** of the income in the **Column Totals** row. To find the **average**, divide the count into the total ($600/4); the resulting average is consistent with the paycheck amounts considering the amount of the paycheck is the same each time.

Be certain to log income like tips each day as you receive them. Money in hand is easy to spend and you want to be sure to record what you have (or had) to work with over the month so that you can take control of it.

With all your income logged on the sheet for the month, calculate your column totals, averages, and counts (the number of entries in that column) at the top of each column. The total for the Bonus 1 column is $462 and the average is $21 ($462/22).

Next, let's figure entries for your **surplus** columns. For the income columns labeled Bonus 1 and Bonus 2 (if you used both), note the average for the column. Find all the entries in the Bonus 1 column that are higher than the column average and calculate the difference (the higher than average amount minus the column average). Enter the difference as a surplus next to the entry in the Surplus 1 column. On the **example**, you'll see nine entries in the **Surplus** 1 column for the number of times that the tips received during the month exceeded the average tip for the 22 days that were worked. Do the same for the Bonus 2 and Surplus 2 columns if you have used them.

With all your bonus income logged and the amounts that exceeded the average income for that activity in the surplus column, add the entries for the Surplus 1 column and enter a column total at the top of the page. Do the same for the Surplus 2 column if you used it. Add the Surplus 1 and 2 totals together and create a habit of depositing that amount into a savings account. Extra money that you have chosen not to spend is your wealth, consider using it to generate more money.

In our **example** we chose to do something slightly different than expected. Since the month was December and the income in the Bonus 2 column was a $150 Christmas bonus from work and $60 of gift money from Christmas cards, we considered it all bonus income and just added it with the **Surplus 1** total of $75 and deposited it all ($285) in savings. Remember, it's your money and you can use it, and the worksheets, however you wish. The key point is that you organize your finances and know where your money is coming from and going to so that you can make informed decisions in how you choose to use it.

Learning to live on the average income from an unpredictable income source allows you to build up a surplus. With surplus funds in reserve in a savings account, months when cash flow isn't so good can be supported with the extra funds that you set aside from earlier months when things were better. Over time as your income averages out, you will likely find that the surplus money in your savings goes unused and you build up a nice amount of money that can be put to use in other places; like paying down debt, creating additional income sources such as investments, or rewarding yourself or your family. Successful investments and business ventures diversify your income and continue to add to your increasing wealth. Continue to expand your financial education so you can identify and take advantage of opportunities.

Notes and Instructions:

- ☐ Label your Month and Year, you don't want to lose track come tax time.
- ☐ On top of the general labels are '**Your Labels**' for where your money comes from.
  - Use Income columns 1 through 3 for regular income like a paycheck from your job.
  - Use **Bonus** columns 1 and 2 to log things like tips and other income that varies in either the amount you earn or how often you might earn it.
  - Leave the **Surplus** columns 1 and 2 for end of the month calculations.
- ☐ Log your Data (throughout the month)
  - Whenever you have income, enter it in the column you labeled for that income source on the day you receive it.
  - If you receive a regular paycheck, you might only have two to four entries in the Income 1 column depending on whether you are paid every week or every two weeks.
- ☐ Calculate your totals and averages (end of the month)
  - Count the number of entries in each column and enter the number in the **Column Count** row at the top of the column.
  - Add all the entries in each column to find the sum and enter the total in the **Column Total** box at the top of the column.
  - For each column, divide the Column Total by the Column Count and enter the result in the Column Average box.
  - Add and total all the **Column Totals** (Income and Bonus columns) and enter your total income for the month in the **Total This Month** box in the top right corner. (do not add any totals from the **Surplus** columns which are grayed out; you'd be counting these dollars twice and you'll show more money than you actually have.)
- ☐ People with intermittent and varied income sources are challenged in budgeting by not being able to predict how much money they'll have to work with. Here you'll track occasional income, bank the extra or surplus, and learn to live on averages. This is the where keeping accurate records pays off big:
  - In the **Bonus 1** column, compare each entry with the **Column Average** amount at the top of the column
  - For every entry that is greater than the Column Average, find the 'difference' (subtract the column average from the Bonus 1 entry for that date) and enter the difference in the **Surplus 1** column on that date. You are keeping track of how much money you made that day over and above your average for that income source this month.
  - Repeat the two steps above for both the **Bonus 2** and **Surplus 2** columns.
  - Total the **Surplus 1 and 2** columns and enter the totals at the top for Column Totals.
  - Add the totals of Surplus 1 and Surplus 2 together and enter the result in **Surplus Income**.
  - Subtract the Surplus Income for the month from your total income for the month and enter the result in the **Adjusted Income** box.
- ☐ Deposit your Surplus Income in savings and pay expenses from your Adjusted Income. When you are short, you'll have your own money to draw from. If you can resist spending it, you'll be growing your own wealth every month.

Month December Year 2005

Multiple Income Monthly Log

This worksheet is dedicated to Kassie, a 2005 grad that asked me to work out a solution for her.

Total This Month:	$1272.00
Surplus Income:	$285.00
Adjusted Income:	$987.00

Column Totals:	$600.00			$462.00	$75.00	$210.00	$45.00
Column Averages:	$150.00			$21.00	$8.33	$105.00	$45.00
Column Count:	4			22	9	2	1
Your Labels:							
Date	Income 1	Income 2	Income 3	Bonus 1	Surplus 1	Bonus 2	Surplus 2
1							
2				$15.00			
3				$12.00			
4							
5	$150.00			$26.00	$5.00		
6				$32.00	$11.00		
7				$22.00	$1.00		
8							
9				$15.00			
10				$12.00			
11							
12	$150.00			$27.00	$6.00		
13				$32.00	$11.00		
14				$17.00			
15							
16				$15.00			
17				$12.00			
18							
19	$150.00			$26.00	$5.00	$150.00	$45.00
20				$35.00	$14.00		
21				$17.00			
22							
23				$17.00			
24							
25						$60.00	
26	$150.00			$19.00			
27				$32.00	$11.00		
28				$17.00			
29				$32.00	$11.00		
30				$18.00			
31				$12.00			

Month Year

Multiple Income Monthly Log

Total This Month:	
Surplus Income:	
Adjusted Income:	

Column Totals:							
Column Averages:							
Column Count:							
Your Labels:							
Date	Income 1	Income 2	Income 3	Bonus 1	Surplus 1	Bonus 2	Surplus 2
1							
2							
3							
4							
5							
6							
7							
8							
9							
10							
11							
12							
13							
14							
15							
16							
17							
18							
19							
20							
21							
22							
23							
24							
25							
26							
27							
28							
29							
30							
31							

Month	Year	Multiple Income Monthly Log	
		Total This Month:	
		Surplus Income:	
		Adjusted Income:	

Column Totals:							
Column Averages:							
Column Count:							
Your Labels:							
Date	Income 1	Income 2	Income 3	Bonus 1	Surplus 1	Bonus 2	Surplus 2
1							
2							
3							
4							
5							
6							
7							
8							
9							
10							
11							
12							
13							
14							
15							
16							
17							
18							
19							
20							
21							
22							
23							
24							
25							
26							
27							
28							
29							
30							
31							

Month	Year	Multiple Income Monthly Log					
					Total This Month:		
					Surplus Income:		
					Adjusted Income:		
Column Totals:							
Column Averages:							
Column Count:							
Your Labels:							
Date	Income 1	Income 2	Income 3	Bonus 1	Surplus 1	Bonus 2	Surplus 2
1							
2							
3							
4							
5							
6							
7							
8							
9							
10							
11							
12							
13							
14							
15							
16							
17							
18							
19							
20							
21							
22							
23							
24							
25							
26							
27							
28							
29							
30							
31							

Month Year

Multiple Income Monthly Log

Total This Month:	
Surplus Income:	
Adjusted Income:	

Column Totals:							
Column Averages:							
Column Count:							
Your Labels:							
Date	Income 1	Income 2	Income 3	Bonus 1	Surplus 1	Bonus 2	Surplus 2
1							
2							
3							
4							
5							
6							
7							
8							
9							
10							
11							
12							
13							
14							
15							
16							
17							
18							
19							
20							
21							
22							
23							
24							
25							
26							
27							
28							
29							
30							
31							

Month Year

Multiple Income Monthly Log

Total This Month:	
Surplus Income:	
Adjusted Income:	

Column Totals:							
Column Averages:							
Column Count:							
Your Labels:							
Date	Income 1	Income 2	Income 3	Bonus 1	Surplus 1	Bonus 2	Surplus 2
1							
2							
3							
4							
5							
6							
7							
8							
9							
10							
11							
12							
13							
14							
15							
16							
17							
18							
19							
20							
21							
22							
23							
24							
25							
26							
27							
28							
29							
30							
31							

Month	Year	Multiple Income Monthly Log	
		Total This Month:	
		Surplus Income:	
		Adjusted Income:	

Column Totals:							
Column Averages:							
Column Count:							
Your Labels:							
Date	Income 1	Income 2	Income 3	Bonus 1	Surplus 1	Bonus 2	Surplus 2
1							
2							
3							
4							
5							
6							
7							
8							
9							
10							
11							
12							
13							
14							
15							
16							
17							
18							
19							
20							
21							
22							
23							
24							
25							
26							
27							
28							
29							
30							
31							

Month Year

Multiple Income Monthly Log

Total This Month:	
Surplus Income:	
Adjusted Income:	

Column Totals:							
Column Averages:							
Column Count:							
Your Labels:							
Date	Income 1	Income 2	Income 3	Bonus 1	Surplus 1	Bonus 2	Surplus 2
1							
2							
3							
4							
5							
6							
7							
8							
9							
10							
11							
12							
13							
14							
15							
16							
17							
18							
19							
20							
21							
22							
23							
24							
25							
26							
27							
28							
29							
30							
31							

Month	Year	Multiple Income Monthly Log					
					Total This Month:		
					Surplus Income:		
					Adjusted Income:		
Column Totals:							
Column Averages:							
Column Count:							
Your Labels:							
Date	Income 1	Income 2	Income 3	Bonus 1	Surplus 1	Bonus 2	Surplus 2
1							
2							
3							
4							
5							
6							
7							
8							
9							
10							
11							
12							
13							
14							
15							
16							
17							
18							
19							
20							
21							
22							
23							
24							
25							
26							
27							
28							
29							
30							
31							

Month	Year	Multiple Income Monthly Log					
				Total This Month:			
				Surplus Income:			
				Adjusted Income:			

Column Totals:							
Column Averages:							
Column Count:							
Your Labels:							
Date	Income 1	Income 2	Income 3	Bonus 1	Surplus 1	Bonus 2	Surplus 2
1							
2							
3							
4							
5							
6							
7							
8							
9							
10							
11							
12							
13							
14							
15							
16							
17							
18							
19							
20							
21							
22							
23							
24							
25							
26							
27							
28							
29							
30							
31							

Month Year

Multiple Income Monthly Log

Total This Month:	
Surplus Income:	
Adjusted Income:	

Column Totals:							
Column Averages:							
Column Count:							
Your Labels:							
Date	Income 1	Income 2	Income 3	Bonus 1	Surplus 1	Bonus 2	Surplus 2
1							
2							
3							
4							
5							
6							
7							
8							
9							
10							
11							
12							
13							
14							
15							
16							
17							
18							
19							
20							
21							
22							
23							
24							
25							
26							
27							
28							
29							
30							
31							

Month Year

Multiple Income Monthly Log

Total This Month:	
Surplus Income:	
Adjusted Income:	

Column Totals:							
Column Averages:							
Column Count:							
Your Labels:							
Date	Income 1	Income 2	Income 3	Bonus 1	Surplus 1	Bonus 2	Surplus 2
1							
2							
3							
4							
5							
6							
7							
8							
9							
10							
11							
12							
13							
14							
15							
16							
17							
18							
19							
20							
21							
22							
23							
24							
25							
26							
27							
28							
29							
30							
31							

Month Year

Multiple Income Monthly Log

Total This Month:	
Surplus Income:	
Adjusted Income:	

Date	Income 1	Income 2	Income 3	Bonus 1	Surplus 1	Bonus 2	Surplus 2
Column Totals:							
Column Averages:							
Column Count:							
Your Labels:							
1							
2							
3							
4							
5							
6							
7							
8							
9							
10							
11							
12							
13							
14							
15							
16							
17							
18							
19							
20							
21							
22							
23							
24							
25							
26							
27							
28							
29							
30							
31							

MULTIPLE INCOME ANNUAL LOG

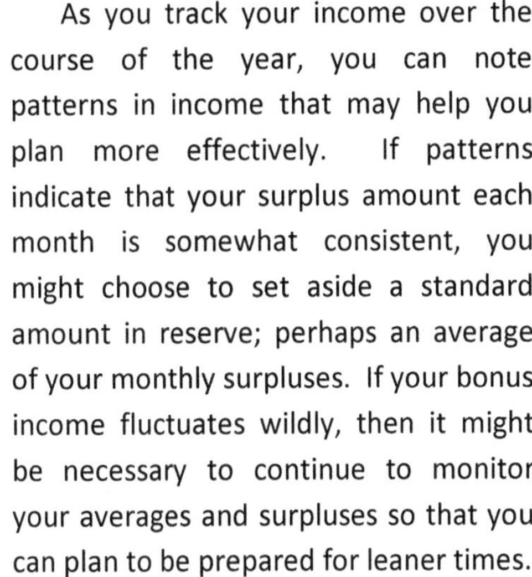

It can be helpful to see and evaluate your annual numbers, a whole year of income on one page to help you plan your budget. The following annual chart was organized to gather information from each month of the **Multiple Income Monthly Log** (Ch. 4) so that you can see and evaluate your income streams and cash flow conveniently.

If you've followed the suggestion of the monthly worksheet and calculated Bonus and Surplus funds as suggested, you'll have both an average amount of money that you can count on from these income sources as well as a surplus of savings from the times you've exceeded your averages from your bonus income. In lean months you can call on these cash reserves to make up for a lower than average income from that income source. If you can be disciplined enough to resist spending this money, or can find other creative ways to limit expenses to cover a shortfall or deficit when you're short, you can continue to save, invest, or reward yourself with your growing wealth.

Once your income levels out, or once you learn to govern your expenses to exist within the confines of your income, monies set aside as a surplus or through a conscious plan to pay yourself first become the seeds for your own personal wealth. You may first accumulate them as a hedge against lean times and over time develop an emergency fund to cover other larger unforeseen circumstances. As your personal wealth grows you can begin to consider other uses for your money such as investment or the seed money for your own business.

As you track your income over the course of the year, you can note patterns in income that may help you plan more effectively. If patterns indicate that your surplus amount each month is somewhat consistent, you might choose to set aside a standard amount in reserve; perhaps an average of your monthly surpluses. If your bonus income fluctuates wildly, then it might be necessary to continue to monitor your averages and surpluses so that you can plan to be prepared for leaner times.

Bear in mind that one of the characteristics that financial institutions consider when reviewing records for your credit report and resulting credit score is your habit of making deposits to a savings account on a regular basis. Successfully developing and continuing this habit not only raises your credit score over time, but lowers interest rates and therefore payments on loans when you do need to finance things. Insurance companies consider your credit worthiness in consideration of rates and good credit scores and can lower your premiums which saves you money. Even some employers are checking credit reports in consideration of employment.

The following worksheet gives you the opportunity to view your annual income stream on one sheet. As long as you have the information in front of you, you can make informed decisions that keep your financial situation under your control.

- ☐ Label your Year and Name; if you run a copy for your accountant at tax time, it's less likely to get lost.
- ☐ On top of the general labels are '**Your Labels**' for where your money comes from. Be certain to match column labels from your monthly worksheets.
  - Use **Income columns 1 through 3** for regular income like a paycheck from your job.
  - Use **Bonus columns 1 and 2** to log things like tips, consulting, or other income that varies in either the amount you earn or how often you might earn it.
  - You'll use the **Surplus column** to total the amount of calculated surplus throughout the year.
- ☐ Log your Data
  - Working from your monthly worksheets, log your income totals from each column of income for each month; Jan-Dec.
  - EX: If you have 2 paychecks for $750 as regular job income under Income 1 for each month, your total for January would be $1500 for Income 1 on your January Multiple Income Log, and you should transfer this total to this Multiple Income Annual Log.
  - Work carefully to be certain you are reading from the correct month and entering values for the correct month.
- ☐ Calculate your totals, averages, and percentages
  - Add all the entries in each column and log the total in the **Column Total** box at the top of the column.
  - For each column, divide the Column Total by 12 (the number of months in a year) and enter the result in the **Column Average** box. Even if you have no income for certain months, this will average this income type out over 12 months so you can plan for it more accurately and eliminate the wide swings in your income.
  - Add and total all the values under Monthly Total and enter your total income for the year in the **Column Total** box under **Annual** in the upper left corner of the top table.
  - Calculate a percentage of your total income for each of your income sources by dividing each **Column Total** under **Income 1**, **Income 2**, etc., by your total income in the **Column Total** box under **Annual**. The result is expressed as a decimal; interpret it as hundredths and log a percentage.
  - EX: $1500 a month in paychecks times 12 months would be $18,000 annually for that one income type. Dividing that income ($18,000) by a total annual of all your incomes, $37,698 for example, would give you 0.48 (forty-eight hundredths) or 48% of your income from the one income source in that column.
- ☐ Double check your math by adding up column totals for Income 1-3, Bonus 1-2, and Surplus, and compare the result to your Annual Column total that you got by adding up monthly income totals. The two numbers, arrived at by different means, should match if you've worked carefully.
  - If the totals don't match, double check your entries and your total math to try and find the figures that are different.
  - Rerun your check

Multiple Income Annual Log

Year

Name

	Annual	Income 1	Income 2	Income 3	Bonus 1	Bonus 2	Surplus
Your Labels:							
Column Total:							
Column Average:							
Percentage:	100%						

	Monthly Total	Income 1	Income 2	Income 3	Bonus 1	Bonus 2	Surplus
Jan							
Feb							
Mar							
Apr							
May							
Jun							
Jul							
Aug							
Sep							
Oct							
Nov							
Dec							

SAVINGS ALLOCATION WORKSHEET

6

Most people who receive income from a job or small business will manage their cash flow using a bank or credit union account. A checking account is most convenient for cash flow as it allows deposits and a number of disbursements from the account in the form of bank drafts, checks, or electronic funds transfers (EFT's) which are not usually limited in number, to pay their expenses. Good money management practices and a solid understanding of how to generate personal wealth dictate two things: 1) spending everything you have will drain your wealth and 2) keeping all your funds in one easily accessible, high-traffic checking account can also encourage you to spend it all; which drains your wealth. Use of a separate account for funds intended for long-term goals, such as a savings account, will help you protect your long-term assets (from yourself if need be) and still allow you to manage your periodic cash flow with your checking account. Two accounts for two different purposes.

Developing a regular savings plan has several beneficial factors. It is the first step in beginning to generate wealth by not spending everything you have. The habit of saving on a regular basis is also recognized by banking and financial institutions as a wealth-building skill and will significantly raise your credit score over time. Savings accounts normally carry a modest interest rate paid out to the saver each month, which, in contrast to inflation, isn't likely to generate profit, but it can slow down the resulting devaluation of your wealth. A primary reason for keeping funds in a savings account is to ease the financial impact of financial emergencies. In the event of the unexpected and financially devastating, you'll have an emergency fund to fall back on. In addition, most people seeing their savings grow and compound are encouraged, motivated, and develop a sense of accomplishment in the fruit of their financial skills; the embodiment of 'a penny saved is a penny earned'.

While forming the habit of diverting funds to a savings account on a regular basis has many good points, it can be difficult to stay on top of the individual purposes for which you set aside these funds when they are all in one lump. If you've reviewed the Financial Goal (Ch. 3) and Monthly Budget (Ch. 2) worksheets in this volume, each helps you plan for the use of your own money for long-term goals. A savings account with a bank (share account with a credit union) is a good option to protect these funds while you collect them for later use. The Savings Allocation Worksheet in this chapter can help you keep track of both the total amount in this one account, and allow you to track the funds and your progress for several different financial goals at one time.

The Totals for the entire sheet are at the top of the page. The center figure on the top line labeled **(+) General Balance** should match the amount that the bank or credit union reports that you have on deposit. While this is where we will end up, it's not where we should start.

Using the Savings Allocation Worksheet

Eight lines down the page is a row across the page with column headers above it starting with **Date**, then **Description**, **Credit**, **Debit**, etc... When you start using this worksheet, you'll start here, likely with a deposit amount for a new account, or with the current balance from your existing savings account like the first line in the example below. List the date, provide a description (such as deposit, or beginning balance) and an amount in the **Credit (+)** column as a place to start. Each time you make a deposit, make another line entry and add the amount to the **Credit (+)** column. If you ever take money out of the account, make a separate entry on another line listing the date, a description (such as what you're using the money for) and make an entry in the **Debit (-)** column. Keep your credits and debits on separate lines with their own specific descriptions.

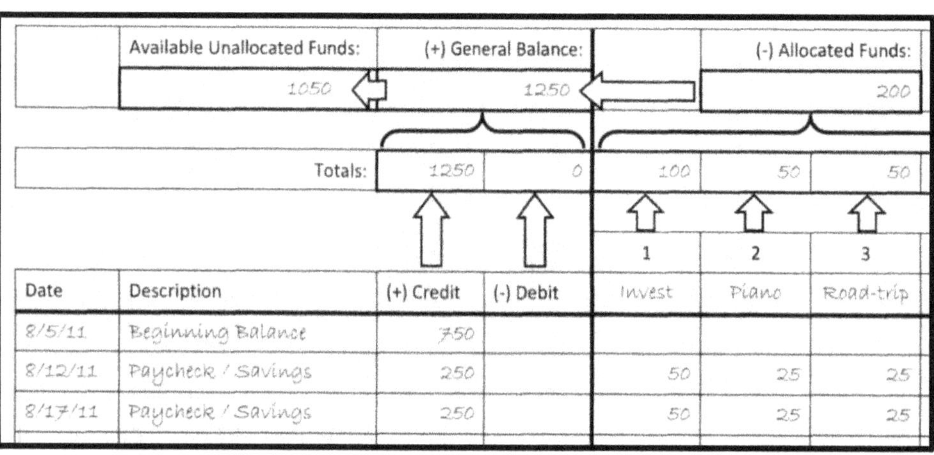

This first section that is LEFT of the heavy column divider is the simple 'unallocated' traffic of funds in your savings account. It's no different than your savings passbook (bank record) and, just like your bank records, shows no difference between dollars for emergencies and dollars for this year's vacation. The dollars for your summer vacation look just like the dollars for your daughter's summer piano lessons.

You can keep track of money for your different goals in the columns to the RIGHT of the heavy column divider in the columns numbered 1 through 6. This is the 'allocated funds' section where you keep track of funds for which you have determined a specific purpose. Under the numbers for these columns is a blank cell in which you can write a short label for the purpose of the column. Vacation, Emergency, Piano; whatever purposes you decide.

As you make a new credit entry for money deposited into the account, $250 for example, you might want to split that amount among several different purposes: $150 for general savings, $50 for future investment, $25 for piano lessons, and $25 for this summer's road-trip. For that entry you'd enter $250 as a **Credit** for all the money being deposited, then split parts of that amount across three more allocated columns: one for investment, one for piano, and one for the road-trip vacation. If you're following closely or making practice entries on the table, you may have noticed we didn't assign $150 of the $250 **Credit** to a numbered allocated column. Since Available Unallocated Funds have no assigned purpose, we won't use an specific column to track it; we'll track it as the difference between the total money in the account and money we've allocated to specific purposes (General Balance minus Allocated Funds).

To keep track of the **General Balance** and the **Allocated Funds**, the second line of cells on the page labeled **Totals** is where we'll add up each column. Start with the **Credit** column and add all the entries in the column and record it in the **Totals** row. Do the same with the **Debit** column. By keeping track of these figures separately you'll have individual figures that show how much total money you have deposited and how much total money you have withdrawn. After a while, the comparison of these two numbers can be quite an education!

On the worksheet we arrive at **General Balance** by subtracting all withdrawals (labeled **Debit**) from all deposits (labeled **Credit**). Your **General Balance** should match the balance calculated by your financial institution on your monthly statement, except for any deposits or withdrawals that you've made in between when the bank drafted your statement and when you received it. Subtracting any outstanding deposits or withdrawals that you made after the bank created your statement should 'reconcile' your account. If the amount still doesn't match what your bank says, dig deeper; matching your deposits and withdrawals to the bank's records to see which of you is missing information. Banks aren't perfect. It's a good idea to keep deposit slips and check your statement or passbook (bank records) to be certain that the records are correct in case you find mistakes when your statement arrives.

When you receive your statement, also be certain to note how much interest you earned that month. Make an entry in your **Credit** column with the description 'interest' so that you keep track of what you are earning from the bank.

Total each of the allocated columns (1-6) and enter a total on the totals row. Then add each of the allocated totals together to find the total for the cell in the first row labeled **Allocated Funds**. This is the total amount in savings for which you've already determined a specific purpose.

In the top row, subtracting the **Allocated Funds** figure from the **General Balance** total (the difference) will give you the amount of money for the **Available Unallocated Funds** cell at the top of the sheet. If you keep your records current, and recalculate the totals rows at the top of the page with each deposit or withdrawal entry, you can tell how much money you have in your savings for each assigned purpose at a glance.

One more calculation will bear some explanation. When you reach your financial total for one of your allocated goals, you'll eventually want to withdraw the money so that you can apply it to your goal and finalize your plan. (Hooray!) When you make the entry for this withdrawal in the Debit column, also make a withdrawal entry from the column for which you allocated that goal. This allows you to reuse that column for another goal and keep the balance of funds in that column accurate since you also removed the funds from that column. Once you've done that, adding up the positives AND the negatives in that column should equate to zero until you start assigning more funds to that column for a new goal and a new purpose. Be sure to make a note in the description column to remind yourself why you withdrew the funds from the account in the **Debit** column as well as the numbered allocated column. Be sure to change your column label for your new allocated goal. Using a pencil will keep your records, certain to need corrections at some point, both neat and easier to correct.

To keep things a bit more clear, and to keep you from having to add up a column full of numbers that will cancel themselves out once a goal has been reached, you can mark out your completed goals in the allocated columns. Since all the allocated funds (+) in a column will cancel out with the removal of funds from that column (-) you can cross out the cells of the chart, or highlight them, or color them in lightly with colored pencil once that goal is completed. If you mark up your chart in this manner, you can quickly tell what part of the column is still active and skip all the calculator work for the cells of the column that are no longer 'active'.

If you are running a business and earning funds for which you'll be logging deductions for income tax purposes, you do want to use an account separate from your personal accounts. Legally, if you intermingle personal and business funds, the law won't distinguish your business financial activity from your personal financial activity. This can have serious and sometimes catastrophic consequences in the event you are sued in connection with your business activity. Since your funds would be intermingled, your personal and business activity are intermingled and your personal assets (home, savings...) could be up for grabs if a settlement goes against you. Consult appropriate legal and tax professionals for the proper use of separate accounts if you are also operating a business.

Next year, when you start a new workbook for your annual finances, you can transfer current totals from this year's log to next year's log. Use 'Current Balance' as the description and log your current balance for each column total. Only transfer the column headers in the allocated (numbered columns) for your current goals. Your completed goals may be reviewed by looking back into the past year's workbook. Start the next year's records with the current balance for each column and continue keeping records as you make new deposits, complete your financial goals, and withdraw money to fund your goals.

For personal accounting, keeping funds for different financial goals in one savings account should simplify your finances in that you only have to deal with one financial institution, one account; one monthly statement. This worksheet should make keeping track of the many goals you have set for that one big ball of money much easier. As a happy little bonus, all the money you have in the account may be earning you a small amount of interest while it's waiting to be put to good use. Having the bank pay for even a small part of your next goal is a very satisfying strategy indeed.

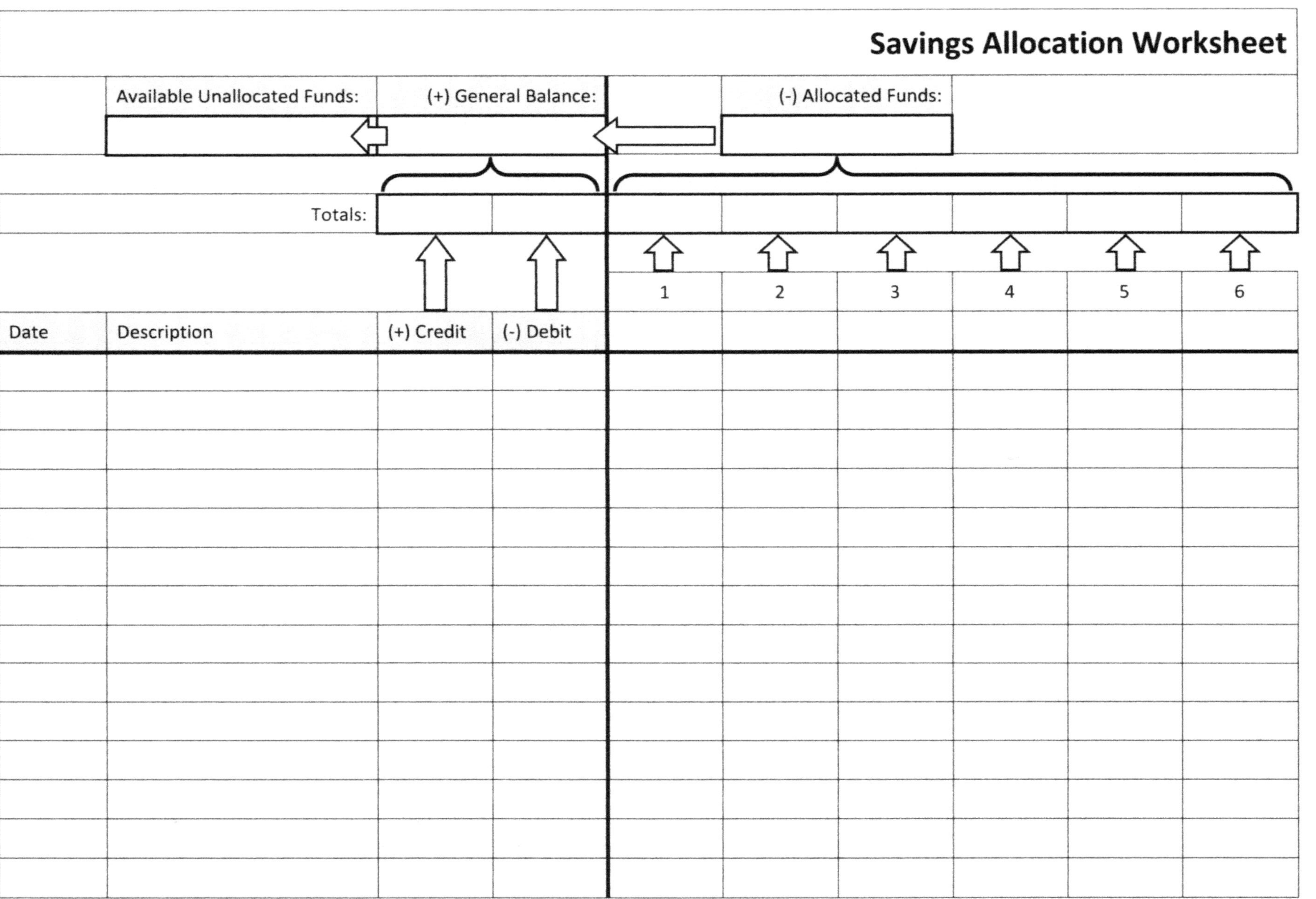

Savings Allocation Worksheet

Available Unallocated Funds: | (+) General Balance: | (-) Allocated Funds:

Totals:									
				1	2	3	4	5	6
Date	Description	(+) Credit	(-) Debit						

Date	Description	(+) Credit	(-) Debit						

Date	Description	(+) Credit	(-) Debit						

Date	Description	(+) Credit	(-) Debit						

7 PIE CHART WORKSHEETS

Some people benefit greatly by seeing a visual chart of their income and/or expenses rather than trying to read and interpret rows and columns of numbers. Seeing how large one element of your budget is in comparison to others can have a significant impact. As stated throughout the text, online resources at mymoneysmart.com are currently under development. It is our intent to publish electronic versions of the worksheets, many of which will include charts that are generated automatically from information that you supply in the worksheets. Utilizing the online service will make much of the work of managing your budget much easier and more convenient. Do check in with us at mymoneysmart.com to make use of the resources as they are completed and become available.

If you've never worked with a chart like this before, the circle or 'pie' represents the whole, or 'all' of something; for our purposes: 100% of your income. Relating the pie charts to the Multiple Income Annual Log you may have worked with in the Chapter 5, Multiple Income Annual Log, all of your income would be broken into sections or 'slices' of pie that relate in size to your other sources of income. Being able to see how physically large or small the slices are in comparison once you've drawn them may give you some additional insight into what you can do with your budget resources.

Another group of information that is a good candidate for a pie chart is the information you may have gathered on the Monthly Cash Flow Worksheet in chapter one. It might be valuable to chart and view both the **Currency** used when you spent money (i.e. cash, debit, credit, etc...), and the **Category** for each (i.e. transport, food, cash, etc...). You would do a separate chart for each set of information (Currency and Category) as they are not directly related.

A pie chart of payment methods might reveal your cash expenses were larger than credit or debit expenses. If that were the case you might ask yourself, "Do I tend to spend more money when I have cash in my pocket?" My father would have said to me, "Money burns a hole in my pocket." If the credit section is significantly larger than cash or debit it might raise the question, "Am I using more credit than I can pay back in one month, and is the interest on that credit costing me more money than I want to lose?" Whatever questions your calculations and pie chart view of the results might raise, those questions may lead you to some very effective changes in your financial habits, if you choose to make them.

Before you can draw a pie chart, you first have to have the data (the numbers) on which the chart is based. If you are working through the MoneySmart™ program on paper, you'll have to spend some time with a calculator to generate those numbers and calculate percentages.

You can draw a simple pie chart by drawing a circle, dividing the circle into quarters, then drawing two more lines to divide the quarters into 8ths. Each slice of the 8-slice pie is 12.5% (100/8). Estimate how large the pie slices would be from your percentages, color in the pie slices and add some labels to represent your columns. It may be helpful to start at 12-O'clock on the circle and work in a clockwise fashion.

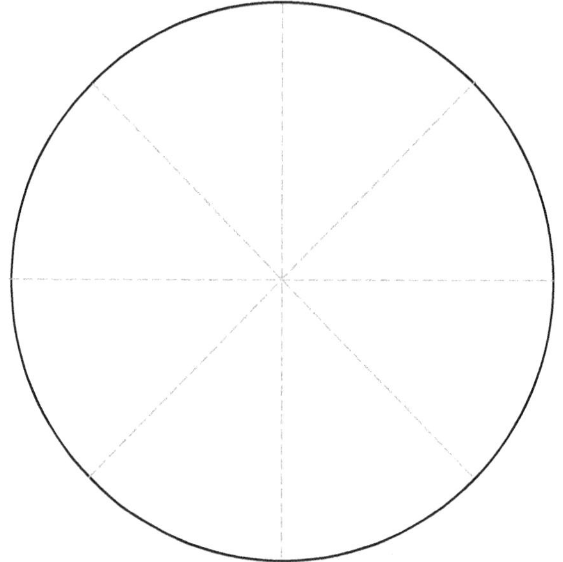

For example, on the circle to the right which is already divided into eight sections, a 10% section of the pie would be slightly smaller than one of the eight sections are at 12.5% each. A 25% section of the pie would be exactly two of the eight sections (or 12.5% x 2), and a 40% section of the pie would be slightly larger than three whole sections of the eight (12.5 x 3 = 37.5 ...and a bit more).

You really don't have to be too accurate with the size of the pie slices as you're only creating the charts for a visual reference. Chances are, if your numbers for different sections are close to the same value, you'll be drawing them about the same size, and if they are different, you'll be drawing them different; and that's really all you're trying to accomplish here. Of course, all of this is completely optional. You are certainly not required to draw charts unless you think it will help you to see your financial *picture* more clearly, well, *as a picture*. I leave it your choice.

KEY

KEY

INVESTMENT POSITION WORKSHEET

8

Some Basic Notes on Investing:

The **Investment Position Worksheet** was included to encourage readers to experiment with tracking stock market and other investment performance. Many people don't have the opportunity to work with this type of financial information in school unless they've taken some business classes. Therefore, a worksheet to organize investment information is included to encourage you to experiment and develop an understanding of how investment vehicles work for you in creating income and financial growth. The more you understand about investing, the better you'll do when deciding where to put the wealth you've created to work. To restate from the disclaimer, it is strongly recommended that you seek the guidance and assistance of a certified financial advisor prior to investing.

There is always an amount of risk in investing, but you can negate some of that risk with research, education, and the help of a good financial advisor that shares your investment philosophy. Before you can find a financial advisor that shares your investment philosophy, you'll need to have an investment philosophy. Its recommend you do some reading and research before putting your hard-earned money on the line. Investing professionals call this 'skin in the game', because if you lose it, it will hurt. The first rule of investing is 'don't lose your capital'.

While you're reading, learning, and studying investing, you can use the following worksheet to experiment and get familiar with how the factors of investing work together to grow your money.

Much can be learned from simply tracking an investment like stock, calculating values, and crunching some numbers.

The two basic strategies discussed here for realizing a profit from investing are Capital Gain (growth) investment or a Cash Flow (income) investment. Each can yield good results but are different enough to warrant their own explanation.

The nature of the stock market and some other types of investments are that their inherent value changes all the time, a characteristic called **volatility**. A volatile market moves up and down and this dynamic change is one part of what makes it possible to profit from the market. In simplest terms, you want to buy something when it is undervalued, and sell it when it is overvalued or 'buy low, and sell high'. How you discern when something is over or under valued is a discussion and book unto itself, and well beyond the scope of what I'm trying to accomplish here: to encourage you to consider generating additional and diverse sources of income which may include investing.

The activity of buying something low and selling it high would result in a taxable event called a **capital gain**. You invested your own money, your 'capital', and intend to pull it out of the market or sell it for more than what you paid for it (a gain in value). Most governments consider this taxable since you realized a profit and therefore income. Buying low and selling high sounds simple enough, only nobody has a crystal ball to see tomorrow's market activity and nobody is ever 100% right in considering what the market is likely to do. It's important to understand the dynamics of the market. 'Not all trees grow to the sky', meaning nothing goes up forever and 'all boats both rise *and fall* with the tide' meaning what goes up also comes down. If this is how you intend to make money in the market, you'll need to have the nerve to ride out market volatility and recognize when to take advantage of opportunities in market highs and lows.

Knowing when to buy or sell also involves knowing the current **market price** (why some traders are glued to their computers or cell phones and what those antique ticker-tape machines were once used for) and knowing your personal **position** on a given stock or investment. Your position is the average price that you paid to hold the shares of stock that you own. As you buy or sell stocks into a constantly moving market and prices move up and down, your position will change depending on a number of factors.

The current market price, the number of shares you are buying at that price, the number of shares you already own, what you had paid for those shares, and any fees incurred in the purchase all affect your position. Yes, that may sound confusing; but it sounds more confusing than it actually is. Simply put, you take the amount of money you've spent to acquire all your shares (including fees, expenses, dividends, and profits) and divide by the number of shares that you own. The result is the average you paid for a share of that stock, or your 'position', which may be higher or lower than the current market price.

While the current market price might be the price at which you can sell or buy more shares, your position is what each share you own is currently worth to you. The calculation does get slightly more complicated when the company is paying a dividend and portions of your capital are coming back to you. These also need to be factored in and we'll cover that in the following paragraphs. The Investment Position Worksheet that organizes all these factors is included in this work so that you can take a look at how investments work, practice with it if you choose, and make more sense of the process. When it comes down to having a conversation with your financial advisor about where your money is invested and how it's performing, you'll be better prepared.

Another way to realize a **yield** (a profit) from your investments is to invest in companies with a history of paying a dividend. **Dividends** are portions of profit from a company that are paid to its shareholders (co-owners) based on the number of shares that they hold. Investing in companies that pay dividends gives you an additional cash flow for as long as you own the stock and the company chooses to pay a dividend. Corporations, like individuals, can take their profits and choose to divide them among shareholders, reinvest them into the company's expansion plans, or pay down debts. Even good companies change their strategies now and then to take advantage of opportunities and may change their dividend policy. Normally more mature and established companies pay dividends and they can and do adjust the dividend up or down depending upon economic climate and company performance. Consistent and rising dividends can be a valuable indicator of a company's performance over time. Companies can't pay out money to shareholders as dividends if they aren't making a consistent profit.

The company will publish or announce a current annual dividend rate, and pay portions of dividends each quarter or every three months. For example, if a company is paying a one dollar ($1.00) annual dividend, you'll likely see twenty-five cents ($0.25) per share issued as a dividend each quarter ($1.00 / 4 = $0.25).

As mentioned earlier, when dividends are paid out to you, your position adjusts slightly as the amount of money you have invested has changed. Some of your money has come back to you, you have recovered a portion of your capital, and it affects the overall price that you have paid for each share. Albeit a small adjustment in some cases, it is wise to know your exact position so that you can make informed decisions on where you stand in reference to the current market price of a stock. Should you wish to **liquidate** (sell) some or all or your shares to take advantage of a good investment opportunity, you'll want to know your precise position so that you can avoid selling shares at less than what you paid for them, if possible.

Many investors reinvest dividends buying additional shares, which increases the number of shares on which they are paid when the dividend is next released. This 'compounding' of their investment allows the investor to earn a return on money that was earned from their capital, thereby earning interest on interest; a very powerful investment strategy.

Parts of the Investment Position Worksheet:

The worksheet is organized into columns to track the factors that directly affect your position, or the value of the shares that you hold. If you are faithful in recording these factors as they change, you can easily run the formulae at the top of the worksheet to figure the value of your holdings. Use a pencil; you may wish to recalculate values A-H as often as every time you add a new event.

The **Capital Gain** factors are of importance when buying and selling shares which may result in a capital gain or capital loss. The section and headers for these factors are highlighted gray.

- **Date** - the date on which the transaction, the purchase, sale, or dividend takes place.
- **Share Price** - the market price per share at the time of your buy or sell event
- **Buy Shares** - how many shares are purchased (column separate from sell shares as with a ledger)
- **Debit Capital** - the total amount of capital or money spent to acquire the shares (share price x buy shares)

Company Name	Ticker	Current Shares [G = A – D]	Current Equity [H = E + F – B – C]	Current Position [X = H / G]
General Electric	GE	G 69	H -497.77	X -7.21

Return On Investment (ROI) is a performance estimate whose value is only valid when calculated with the most current Dividend Rate (R), Shares Paid (S) and Equity (H) values ROI = S(4R)/H

Totals →	A 155	B $2087.90	C $35.03	D 86	E $1553.16		Total →	F $72.00
	↑	↑	↑	↑	↑			↑

Date	Share Price	Buy Shares	Debit Capital (-)	Comm/Fee (-)	Sell Shares	Credit Capital (+)	Dividend Rate (R)	Shares Paid (S)	Received
10/20	19.80	25	495.00	7.00					
1/26							0.31	25	7.75
4/27							0.31	25	7.75
5/13	12.98	75	973.50	7.00					
6/22	11.27	20	234.40	7.00					
6/22	11.55	10	115.50	7.00					
7/8	10.78	25	269.50	7.00					
7/27							0.10	100	10.00
10/26							0.10	155	15.50
1/25							0.10	155	15.50
3/19	18.06			0.02	67	1210.02			
3/19	18.06			0.01	19	343.14			
4/26							0.10	155	15.50

- **Commission/Fee** (Comm/Fee) - any commission or fee that you incurred through a broker for a buy or sell event. ($5-35 is common)
- **Sell Shares** - how many shares are sold (column separate from buy shares as with a ledger)
- **Credit Capital** - the total amount of capital or money recovered through sale of shares (share price x sell shares)

The **Cash Flow** or income factors are important with companies that are paying a dividend. As not all companies pay dividends, these factors are listed in the section off to the right and the headers are clear or white rather than gray.

- **Dividend Rate** - the amount of money that the company is paying out for each share this quarter. You'll receive a statement and this will be listed with the dividend event.
- **Shares Paid** - the number of qualifying shares you owned at the time of the dividend. Shareholders must own the shares for a significant portion of the previous quarter to qualify to receive dividends on those shares. If you bought shares late in the quarter, you may not qualify to earn a dividend on those shares until the following quarter.
- **Received** - the total amount of the dividend you received (= dividend rate x shares paid)
- **Comm/Fees** - there are sometimes commissions, fees, or taxes assessed on dividends, as with shares of foreign companies. Use the Comm/Fees column to track these.

The top section of the worksheet is the result of your data and calculations. You'll refigure these values each time you have a need to know your precise position. Those independent thinkers among you that by this time are still using a pen, might wish to review Chapter 3, where you can map out a plan to buy a pencil. ☺

- **Current Shares** - how many shares you currently own [= buy shares (A) – sell shares (B)]
- **Current Equity** - the total amount of money you paid to own these shares, including fees, minus the amount of capital recovered through dividends and sale of shares.
- **Current Position** - the average price you've paid to own each share considering shares bought, shares sold, fees paid, dividends received, and divided by the current amount of shares you currently own.
- **ROI** - return on investment; the performance of this investment in returning your original capital to you, calculated as an annual rate similar to the APR (annual percentage rate) of a savings account. The ROI indicates how quickly your investment will return your original capital to you and in effect, 'pay for itself'.

Using the Investment Position Worksheet:

Each time you create an event with your chosen stock: a purchase, a sale, a dividend payout, a split; you should make an entry on your worksheet. These 'events' will allow you to track the information and be able to use the factors to accurately calculate your current values. Not all events (a purchase, sale, or dividend) will use all the columns so there will be blanks. As long as you're working on paper, you'll need to calculate and recalculate the results, so use pencil.

When you initiate a **stock purchase**, you list the date, the market price at which you acquired the shares (**share price**), and the number of shares you purchased (**buy shares**). From those factors you can calculate the total amount of capital you paid for the shares (**debit capital**) through multiplying the share price by the number of shares. You can find the precise commission or fee for the transaction at the time of the sale, or listed in your account statement which your broker will make available.

One strategy to acquire additional shares is known as '**Dollar Cost Averaging**'. The strategy is simple, effective, and tends to remove the influence of emotion in response to market volatility. Dollar cost averaging is establishing the personal discipline to apply a fixed amount of money to buying stock (or other assets) at a set interval regardless of the value of the stock in the market at that time. Since the dollar amount is fixed, that amount of money purchases more shares when the stock value is down, and less shares when the stock value is up. Buying stock in this manner tends to average out a great deal of the market volatility over time.

'**Buying on Dips**' is another strategy in which the investor holds back their investment dollars in anticipation that the stock price will drop below their current position price and they can buy 'on sale'. Acquiring more shares at a lower price with more money can reduce your position significantly. This method can yield much less predictable results as the market is difficult to 'time' for dips. Sitting on cash that's doing nothing because it's not in a climbing market, or 'Sitting on the Sidelines' can be nerve wracking.

Many investors use a combination of these methods in that they commit an amount of money to dollar cost averaging, but maintain an increasing amount of 'dry powder' in reserve over time that can be used to acquire more shares if the market price takes a favorable turn. The dollar cost average ensures that they are in the market to take profits when good, and the money held in reserve ensures that they can take advantage of market opportunity if and when good stocks dip in price.

Sale of Stock is a mirror of the factors involved in a stock purchase. There are a number of shares sold, at a specific market price, with a commission fee on a particular date. Again, this account activity with your broker will be an event that will show up in your account records and on your account statement. Be sure to log the shares sold in the **Sell Shares** column and the amount of capital recovered in the **Credit Capital** column. Since fees for each transaction are always negative, you use the same **Comm/Fees** column for a sale as you would for a purchase.

Selling shares at a profit will return an amount of capital to you and will reduce the amount of capital 'tied up' in the shares you still hold if you did not sell them all. **Taking some money off the table** or **taking profits** is common when the market has increased significantly and the investor can take a capital gain but doesn't want to completely abandon their investment in an otherwise good company. These entries on the worksheet will allow you to take into consideration the capital recovered and figure them into the average of what you paid for the shares you still hold and calculate the profit or loss that resulted from your buying and selling.

When you receive **Dividends**, the company sends a payout to your broker and the funds are credited to your broker account which you can either reinvest, transfer, or withdraw for use elsewhere. Again, this event is recorded by your broker and is available in your account history and on your statement. On the worksheet, enter the event details: the **Dividend Rate**, the number of **Shares Paid** to you with this dividend, and the total dollar amount **Received** in the appropriate columns.

Tracking the information for these events will allow you to total the columns to the top of the page in the cells labeled (A) through (F). This information will allow you to calculate the performance of your investment.

Current Shares is simply the number of shares you've purchased minus the number of shares you've sold (A minus D).

Current Equity, or the value of your holdings, is a combination of capital gain or credit capital (E) plus dividends paid (F), minus the capital you invested (B), minus all commissions and fees (C).

Your **Current Position** is the current equity (H) divided by the number of shares (G) that you currently hold. This number, on which you'll consider buying and selling, is the result of all the other calculations, so work carefully.

ROI is a bit more involved, but indicates the performance of your investment. Multiply the value of the current quarterly dividend by 4 (convert to an annual rate), multiply that by the number of shares for which you were paid the dividend, then divide that total by your Current Equity (H). The result is a decimal whose first two columns can be read as hundredths, or interpreted as a percentage. If your ROI is 0.10 or 10%, it will take you 10 years to recover your initial capital (10% x 10 years = 100%), at which time the investment, which may still be paying dividends, is free!

Applying these techniques and methods for tracking your investments works for assets other than stocks. All assets move up and down in value, display volatility, and can be invested in for gain based on your knowledge, skill, and experience with investing. Once again, it is strongly recommended that you seek the guidance and assistance of a certified financial advisor prior to investing.

The Investing Exercise:

Choose a popular public company, like General Electric (ticker: GE) or Pfizer (ticker: PFE), both companies who at the time of this writing, are paying a dividend. This will allow you to track both the market values for a capital investment and the dividend yield for a cash flow investment. Decide how many entries you'd like to calculate for your own educational benefit. One entry per month will give you 16 entries and a very superficial look at what happens with an investment. Twelve entries for instance on the first of the month, and 4 entries for the dividend awarded each quarter. Tracking this information each week, on close of the market each Friday for instance, would give you 28 entries over 6 months: 26 for each Friday, and again, 2 entries for the dividend awarded each quarter.

Once you've decided how many entries you're willing to log on the worksheet, go to Yahoo.com or Google and find their free finance page. You can look up the company's summary by entering the ticker symbols (GE, PFE, or a company of your choosing) in the search window. Adjust the chart information if necessary to look at market values from 12 months ago. The numbers indicated are usually the daily 'close' or market values when trading stopped for that day. Decide how much money you'll give yourself to invest, a lump sum or a budget of a set amount each month, and make hypothetical (imaginary) purchase decisions by logging the information on the worksheet. Look at the next date in the chart at the interval you chose, and decide, 'do I buy or sell?' considering the market price on that date and your current position. Make yourself do one or the other, remember, this is just an exercise. Don't forget to log a commission of $10-15 for the transaction, which you will incur whether you bought or sold. Resist the urge to 'peek ahead'; you don't get to do that when your real money is on the line! Make a game of it and set a dollar amount and time frame with your family members or friends.

One step beyond: choose a sector of the market, such as pharmaceuticals or tele-communications and challenge a friend or family member to find a better company than you to invest in, limiting your choice to a company within that sector. Set a capital amount to invest, a time frame, and see who can find a better company and generate more profit.

Two steps beyond: choose one company and challenge a friend or group of friends to see who can engineer more profits from that one company while tracking acquisition and liquidation activity within a given time frame with a set amount of capital. Then you have only your wits and skills available to help you win!

Good luck, and have fun.

Company Name	Ticker	Current Shares [G = A – D]	Current Equity [H = E + F – B – C]	Current Position [X = H / G]
		G	H	

Return On Investment (ROI) is a performance estimate whose value is only valid when calculated with the most current Dividend Rate (R), Shares Paid (S) and Equity (H) values ROI = S(4R)/H

	Totals →	A	B	C	D	E		Total →	F
		↑	↑	↑	↑	↑			↑
Date	Share Price	Buy Shares	Debit Capital (-)	Comm/Fee (-)	Sell Shares	Credit Capital (+)	Dividend Rate (R)	Shares Paid (S)	Received

Date	Share Price	Buy Shares	Debit Capital (-)	Comm/Fee (-)	Sell Shares	Credit Capital (+)	Dividend Rate	Shares Paid	Received

Company Name	Ticker	Current Shares [G = A – D]	Current Equity [H = E + F – B – C]	Current Position [X = H / G]
		G	H	

Return On Investment (ROI) is a performance estimate whose value is only valid when calculated with the most current Dividend Rate (R), Shares Paid (S) and Equity (H) values — ROI = S(4R)/H

Totals →	A	B	C	D	E	Total →	F
	↑	↑	↑	↑	↑		↑

Date	Share Price	Buy Shares	Debit Capital (-)	Comm/Fee (-)	Sell Shares	Credit Capital (+)	Dividend Rate (R)	Shares Paid (S)	Received

Date	Share Price	Buy Shares	Debit Capital (-)	Comm/Fee (-)	Sell Shares	Credit Capital (+)	Dividend Rate	Shares Paid	Received

Company Name	Ticker	Current Shares [G = A – D] G	Current Equity [H = E + F – B – C] H	Current Position [X = H / G]
Return On Investment (ROI) is a performance estimate whose value is only valid when calculated with the most current Dividend Rate (R), Shares Paid (S) and Equity (H) values				ROI = S(4R)/H

	Totals →	A	B	C	D	E		Total →	F
		↑	↑	↑	↑	↑			↑
Date	Share Price	Buy Shares	Debit Capital (-)	Comm/Fee (-)	Sell Shares	Credit Capital (+)	Dividend Rate (R)	Shares Paid (S)	Received

Date	Share Price	Buy Shares	Debit Capital (-)	Comm/Fee (-)	Sell Shares	Credit Capital (+)	Dividend Rate	Shares Paid	Received

Company Name	Ticker	Current Shares [G = A – D]	Current Equity [H = E + F – B – C]	Current Position [X = H / G]
		G	H	

Return On Investment (ROI) is a performance estimate whose value is only valid when calculated with the most current Dividend Rate (R), Shares Paid (S) and Equity (H) values — ROI = S(4R)/H

	Totals →	A	B	C	D	E		Total →	F
		↑	↑	↑	↑	↑			↑

Date	Share Price	Buy Shares	Debit Capital (-)	Comm/Fee (-)	Sell Shares	Credit Capital (+)	Dividend Rate (R)	Shares Paid (S)	Received

Date	Share Price	Buy Shares	Debit Capital (-)	Comm/Fee (-)	Sell Shares	Credit Capital (+)	Dividend Rate	Shares Paid	Received

Company Name	Ticker	Current Shares [G = A – D]	Current Equity [H = E + F – B – C]	Current Position [X = H / G]
		G	H	

Return On Investment (ROI) is a performance estimate whose value is only valid when calculated with the most current Dividend Rate (R), Shares Paid (S) and Equity (H) values — ROI = S(4R)/H

	Totals →	A	B	C	D	E		Total →	F
		↑	↑	↑	↑	↑			↑
Date	Share Price	Buy Shares	Debit Capital (-)	Comm/Fee (-)	Sell Shares	Credit Capital (+)	Dividend Rate (R)	Shares Paid (S)	Received

Date	Share Price	Buy Shares	Debit Capital (-)	Comm/Fee (-)	Sell Shares	Credit Capital (+)	Dividend Rate	Shares Paid	Received

CONCLUSIONS

If you've taken the time and put forth the effort to use the materials in this book as suggested, you have taken a close look at your personal financial habits, identified areas worthy of your attention, and perhaps you've decided to make some changes in your financial habits. You should have committed your income and monthly expenses to writing so that you can monitor them and consider their effectiveness in your overall financial plan. If you've been working with your budget over more than a few months, I'm certain that you now see and will continue to see opportunities for more effective management of your own money.

If your intent in beginning this journey was to find ways to eliminate debt, I hope that you have made some progress and are encouraged by the progress you are making to further reduce your debt load. As you continue to pay down debts, you'll see more of your money come under your own control to be used to pay down other debts in larger portions. That is a level of financial power that can be seen early as debts begin to melt away with a concentrated effort. I hope that you now realize, that the more debt you remain under, the more you surrender financial control of your efforts and assets to someone else. As you reduce your debt load to more manageable levels, putting money to work on more useful personal goals like retirement, your child's education, or a rewarding family vacation can be a poignant source of pride and personal satisfaction.

In contrast to what many may think, not all debt is bad debt. Robert Kiyosaki, author of the popular Rich Dad, Poor Dad series of publications, admits he 'loves' his credit cards. I doubt, however, that he would recommend that you finance 'doodads' (his word for items you don't really need) with consumer credit. The fact is that some credit is necessary. Many people wouldn't be able to afford to buy a house, a car, or invest in a business that employs and provides jobs for other people if it weren't for our credit system. Good debt is that debt from which you can see a significant benefit, like the roof over your head, or something from which you can achieve profit, such as a profitable business venture. Handling debt responsibly also raises your credit score resulting in lower interest rates, lower payments when you do use credit, and lower premiums for necessary expenses like mortgages and insurance. For years I've said to my students, 'credit cards and chain saws are both good tools, and each will cost you an arm and a leg if you don't know how to use them properly'. Be wise in your credit decisions and reduce your debt load to a level that you can handle responsibly.

Perhaps debt reduction was not your initial motivation. My personal interest in getting control over my finances was to generate enough wealth to seed investments that could supplement and eventually replace my normal income. It can be very motivating to see money that you've worked for, that you've chosen to set aside for a purpose, begin to multiply.

As you create the habit of paying yourself first, savings get noticeably larger and larger over the months and other doors begin to open. Emergency expenses take less of a toll on your nerves as money in the savings account softens otherwise financially devastating news. Desires for a better lifestyle come to fruition as the means to pay for the steps that take you there can be financed from your own money rather than having to pay a premium in interest for everything you do. Poor credit scores begin to climb as money in savings accumulates, good habits of saving are a matter of record, debt loads are reduced, and payments are back on schedule. When credit scores are higher, insurance rates and interest rates (when debt does become necessary) are usually lower, saving you more money. As your personal wealth increases, opportunities to invest in larger ventures open up. Stock market, initial public offerings (shares made available before the general public can get involved), commercial real estate, business partnerships, limited partnerships, all come into consideration as the efforts you've put forth in generating your own capital, your own wealth, qualify you to participate in better investments.

Where you choose to go from here with your new money management skills is up to you. If you saved for retirement, managing what you've saved will be key in making it last for the duration of your retirement and all the uncertainties therein. If you're intent is to own your own business, then you'll certainly need financial management skills to stay in business. If your intent is to generate enough money from investments that your investments become self-sustaining, you'll certainly need the beginning of a financial education that you've started here to be wise enough to make good investment decisions. And if you love your job, as some people do, then managing expenses and income from a company that decides how much money you will be paid each month will continue to be critical in applying limited resources (however generous) to your personal needs. Whatever the next steps in your journey are, I hope that the information I've organized here has either given you a clear and well-lighted path for your first financial steps, or given you valuable ideas so that your walk to financial success can become a steady and determined run. I do hope that you have enjoyed the journey thus far, and I pray that you'll be blessed with much success.

About the Author:

When I was about 16 years old, I sat with my drum teacher Joe Parlink, and after studying with him for about 2 years he said to me, 'You should consider teaching, you're starting to get good at this; when you teach, you learn more." From his encouragement, I began to look for young students who were just starting to learn to play drums, and I've had some form of income or have been seeking some form of income from sources other than a job ever since. At one point I was teaching at three different music stores as well as hosting students at home, I played in two bands, and was an assistant band director with a public high school in Ohio. I had even authored a book on the subject of drumming (another foray into income diversification) which received favorable reviews from a leading trade magazine. When my interests turned to photography, I sought employment in the private sector as a lab technician, but also used my skills as a photographer with the United States Marine Corps Reserve, serving with the only reserve photo unit in the Marine Corps at that time. Later I worked with photography in sales and in addition to serving retail customers, I took freelance jobs as a photographer for clients and taught classes in photography at local college campuses and trade schools.

Over the past decade, I saw the opportunity to teach photography full-time in the public school system and came to Arizona where I was immersed in the Career and Technical Education system. Being CTE certified I expanded my teaching areas to Business and have been teaching business classes to high school students for nearly a decade. This literary work stems from my involvement with high school students who were required to be employed as a component of an Internship program. Many of these students were employed and dealing with both cash flow and expenses for the first time in their lives. It wasn't long before I concluded that to teach students how to find jobs and get themselves hired and not to teach them how to manage their finances was simply negligent. From this perception I began to organize and author solutions and training exercises to help my students understand that while they were currently working for money, they should have a plan to 'have money work for them'; sooner rather than later.

It has been an inspiring time working with my young students and I found I very much enjoyed sharing with them what I had learned about managing finances, budgeting, and investing while I worked with them on class curriculum. This work stems from numerous Parents' reaction to the parent night presentation of what I was sharing with their students throughout the term. The question, 'Can I take your class?' from parent after parent was more than a subtle hint that there might be more people interested in just such a body of information. I perceived that beyond the few hundred students I could contact each year, that there were many more people who may benefit from an organized system of tools to manage their finances. In 2010, I began to organize my charts and exercises into one volume for publication.

My hopes for this work are that it helps clear up confusion in budgeting, helps you to organize your financial information, and that it reduces your workload in creating a budget. In doing so, those who work with this system may begin to see possibilities to reduce debt loads, begin to build personal wealth, and begin to seek opportunities for additional sources of income like investments or their own businesses. I pray it serves you well; best wishes.

Resources, Recommended Reading, and Additional Study

"Creating S.M.A.R.T. Goals." *Goal Setting.* Top Achievement, Self Improvement and Personal Development Community. n. d. Web. August 27, 2011.

"Financial Planning Process." *Learn About Financial Planning.* Certified Financial Planner Board of Standards, Inc. 2011. Web. September 4, 2011.

Clason, George S. *The Richest Man in Babylon*. New York, New York. Signet. Print.

Kiyosaki, Robert and Sharon L. Lechter. *Cashflow Quadrant, Rich Dad's Guide to Financial Freedom.* New York: Warner Business Books. Print.

----. *Rich Dad, Poor Dad; What the Rich Teach Their Kids About Money – That the Poor and Middle Class Do Not!*. New York: Warner Business Books. Print.

Maloney, Michael. *Guide to Investing in Gold and Silver.* New York, Boston: Business Plus. Print.

Allen, C. W. 'Al', with Cheri S. Hill, Diane Kennedy CPA, Garrett Sutton Esq. *Inc. & Grow Rich!* Reno, NV: Sage International, Inc. Print.

Graham, Benjamin. *The Intelligent Investor.* New York, HarperCollins Publishers. Print.

National Endowment for Financial Education. *NEFE High School Financial Planning Program, Student Guide.* Greenwood Village, CO: National Endowment for Financial Education. Print.

Fergusson, Niall. *The Ascent of Money.* New York, New York: The Penguin Press. Print (Also available on DVD as a series)

Frontline. *The Card Game.* PBS Video. 2009. PBS. 2009. http://video.pbs.org/video/1342007771

Financial Sense Newshour – Financial Sense. 2011. Financial Sense. 1987-2012. Web.

King World News Broadcast – King World News. 2011. King World News. 2011. Web.

Afterburner and *Firewall* commentary series – Declaration Entertainment. 2012 Declaration Entertainment. 2012. Web (video)

Scottrade- Knowledge Center. 2011. Scottrade. 2011. Web.

Yahoo! Finance - Investing. 2010. Yahoo!. 2010. Web

www.ingramcontent.com/pod-product-compliance
Lightning Source LLC
Chambersburg PA
CBHW051222200326
41519CB00025B/7208
9780615585086